THE QUALITARIAN

by Dez Stephens

Paperclip Publishing, LLC
Chandler, AZ

The Qualitarian

Copyright © 2022 by Dez Stephens

Published by: Paperclip Publishing LLC

Editor: Nathan Miller
Cover Design: Keenan S. Peebles
Interior Typography: Hannah Thigpen

Library of Congress Control Number: 2022939000

ISBN: 979-8-88589-196-7 (paperback)

ISBN: 979-8-88589-195-0 (hardcover)

ISBN: 979-8-88589-197-4 (eBook)

Printed in Rephen Printing, Co. LTD in Guangzhou and the United States of America

First Printing: 2022

Paperclip Publishing LLC
3800 W Ray Road Suite 5
Chandler, AZ 85226

www.paperclippublishing.com

TO KENT,
who lived more fully in one day than most people do in an entire lifetime

Contents

Introduction

Becoming a professional life coach in 2005 changed everything for me. It was the turning point in my career where everything started falling into place. Coaching found me, not the other way around. And I am so grateful it did.

Back in 2003, a colleague surprised me by saying, "You would make an incredible life coach!" My response was, "Why me?" She answered, "You're so resourceful and compassionate." After a moment I said, "But I'm not a very good listener." She smiled. "You'll learn how to listen if you go to a professional training school."

Honestly, this is what hooked me. Because I knew I struggled with listening. I'd walk away from lunch with a friend feeling empty—because I did the majority of the talking. Rarely did I learn what was going on in someone else's life.

Like a fish to water, I dove into my coach certification training. How could I have missed that this was my destiny? I had considered counseling, teaching and nursing—but never coaching. I was thrilled! I finally found my calling.

Since then, during my decade and a half of professional coaching, I have learned to lean into the quality of life among my clients. This has led me to the concept of *Living as a Qualitarian*.

QUALITARIAN QUIZ

Ask yourself the following questions to gauge how much of a *Qualitarian* you are before reading this book:

1. When you dine out and look at the menu, are you reading left to right or right to left? In other words, are you making your decision based on price or ordering what you really want?

2. When breaking up with someone, do you take the time and energy to end things well or do you tend to avoid the conflict of it?

3. When you're alone at home, are you busying yourself or truly enjoying your home time?

4. Are you more of a be-er or do-er?

5. When you travel, are you taking advantage of opportunities like dining in a new place or walking new streets? Or are you dreading the travel itself?

6. When you take a shower or a bath, are you going through the motions or are you mindful of your senses?

7. When you go for a walk, do you notice the sun and the wind in your face? Are you looking up?

8. When you know it's a new or full moon, do you go outside and look up into the sky?

9. When you feed yourself, are you also nourishing yourself?

10. If you're introverted, do you unnecessarily push yourself to be with others? If you're extroverted, are you surrounding yourself with positive people or just people in general?

11. Is your sex life satisfying or routine?

12. Is your language uplifting when it comes to others? How is your inner voice?

13. Do you feel connected to something larger than yourself?

14. Are you savoring special moments with loved ones or going through the motions?

15. How do you feel when you spend money? Do you feel differently when you spend money on yourself?

16. What do you love about your body? Can you appreciate it?

17. Would you say your mind is calm or chaotic?

18. Are your spaces cluttered or ordered? Are you comfortable with your spaces?

19. Are you fully feeling your feelings?

20. Is your career on track or stuck in a rut?

21. Are your friendships lively or on auto pilot?

22. Does your trusted family know how much you care about them?

These are simple ideas to consider before diving into this book about how I see *Qualitarianism*. You will have plenty more ideas as we go along. No matter how you answer these questions, enjoy the journey!

PART ONE:
PHYSICAL

1

French Women Don't Forget to Eat Chocolate

Most of us love the taste of chocolate. Some freaks don't like it at all—those, "I'm not a sweets person," people. Some of us prefer milk chocolate and some fall in the dark-chocolate-or-nothing category. Either way, chocolate is a highly sensual experience for most of us. There's this moment of enjoyment when you fully succumb to the flavor and texture and mouth-feel.

Surprisingly, some of us are not tasting the chocolate at all. We are grabbing a Snickers bar from the vending machine at work for a quick boost of energy. We are shoving a "shareable" bag of M&Ms in our mouth because we waited too long to eat or we're watching TV or TikTok. We "like chocolate" but are not fully in the experience of enjoying the chocolate.

I imagine that French women or European women or Swiss women appreciate eating chocolate more than most—maybe in places where chocolate or cacao is revered. It's really about mindset—yes, a mindset about chocolate.

Chocolate is a daily staple for me, not just because it tastes great. My soul craves it and my nervous system seems to enjoy it. Maybe it's my French ancestry. Who knows.

Yes, I've learned a bit about our biochemical response when eating chocolate. But it's more of a spiritual experience for me. I'm guessing it has something to do with the sacred cacao where it originates from. Or perhaps that it's so grounding to the body. But I can't eat a Hershey's kiss anymore; I've become a chocolate snob. I'm not talking about the super-expensive kind where six pieces come in a $20 box. I'm also not talking about eating only high-percentage dark chocolate.

For me, eating chocolate like a *Qualitarian* means getting the bars that I really like and thoroughly savoring each piece I eat. My preference is Vosges chocolate—made in Chicago, my hometown. If you love chocolate and haven't yet heard of them—you're welcome! Yes, you can purchase expensive boxes online from their company, but I buy their bars at the supermarket—especially when they're on sale. The quality is so exquisite and the way the chocolate bar breaks when you snap it are just two of the many reasons I love this chocolate and this company. Its owner, Katrina Markoff, is unapologetic about her pricing. I love this about her. She knows the quality she brings and what it takes to provide such consistent quality in her products. Katrina even has yoga + chocolate workshops where you put a piece of their chocolate in your mouth at the end of class as you're lying in Savasana, relaxing and integrating your practice. Such extreme pleasure!

Ask yourself, "What would I ask for as my last meal?" Then consider how you would eat it. Would you scarf it down the way we sometimes do? Would you enjoy every mouthful, every fragrance, every sensation and every bite? I'm guessing the latter. So, what's the difference between this and all of your other meals?

What if you tasted all the bites and every meal with fervor? What if every day could bring you this kind of satisfaction? Imagine anticipating every meal and then actually enjoying every meal. Many of us look forward to eating. Each morning I often think, "I get to eat three yummy meals today." I love food. I love to eat. I love to cook. I love to dine out. This brings me tremendous pleasure in my life.

You might feel otherwise. Many of us anticipate great meals or snacks or desserts. But then we eat them really fast—or we eat them without paying much attention. Suddenly, the meal or moment is over—and feels short-lived. Some of us then go into a state of I-wish-I-didn't-eat-that. We feel anxiety or eagerness beforehand, numbness during, and regret afterward. This is not natural. But it has become our normal.

What if you decided to become a *Qualitarian*—sort of like becoming a vegetarian? Maybe you would start choosing quality ingredients or quality eating establishments. Just like any other form of eating, it's a choice. A choice to decipher whether what you're eating is "quality" in your opinion.

This is not about more-expensive food being higher in quality. It could be. Maybe it should be—but that's not the point. The point is to focus on the highest quality "whatever" in your environment and within your means. Most important, it's about what you decide is quality.

Many studies show that people can get sick when they eat food that they think is bad for them—no matter what the food actually is. Some studies show that people are healthy even when they eat unhealthy foods. It seems to depend on whether they think the food they're eating is actually healthy for them.

Part of this *Qualitarian* lifestyle includes the quality of the company you keep while preparing food or dining out. If you go on a date and don't like your date, the food doesn't taste as good. It won't be as enjoyable if you're stressing about how much the meal costs. Have you ever tried to enjoy food when you're really hungry? It's not easy. It's hard to even taste it.

Think of some of your favorite meals. For me, it might be medium-rare salmon with asparagus—or anything Italian! Do you enjoy these meals more than others? Ask yourself, "Why?" Now consider the possibility that you could equally enjoy eating anything else you routinely eat. Even ramen noodles.

One night, after working a very long day, I remember loving the taste of my ramen noodles. My reasons were twofold. First, I was super hungry. And food typically tastes amazing when we're hungry. Second, I was in this interesting place of appreciation. I was grabbing a quick bite because I needed something fast and easy. But suddenly I was drawn back into a memory of me eating ramen noodles a lot during college.

"Dad, I'm so hungry! I'm only eating ramen noodles because I'm so broke." That's what I told my dad over the phone—four hours from home. I was one of those "starving artist" dance majors who wasn't a big fan of dorm food. So I ate lots of salads and lots of ramen—especially during my first year on campus at the University of Iowa. I was basically calling my dad to beg him to send me some money for some "good food." Looking back now, I reminisce about how fun it was to be in college and learn how to feed myself for the first time.

Now this appreciation brings me joy when I choose to have a bowl of ramen. It really ramps up when I go to a fancy ramen restaurant. See, it's all about perception. Am I disappointed right now (while I'm eating) that it's only ramen noodles? Or am I delighted that I have food when others don't? Am I tasting every bite? Or am I mindlessly eating?

Speaking of my dad, it's because of him that I have an extra appreciation for Italian food and ice cream. My biological dad was my "Sunday Dad." I lived with my mom and stepdad during the week and spent Sundays or some weekends with my dad and stepmom. I wasn't even a year old when my parents split, so this was my normal routine along with my twin sister, Nese.

When we were super young, my dad would take us to the Lincoln Park Zoo or somewhere else fun in Chicago. He was often accompanied by one of his many gorgeous girlfriends. We'd usually eat dinner at some great little Italian restaurant and have spaghetti-and-meatballs or lasagna. Better yet: we'd go to Buffalo Restaurant & Ice Cream Parlor on Irving Park Road in my neighborhood. There were little jukeboxes at each wood-carved booth and sundaes piled high with real whipped cream and one of those great cookie wafers with a cherry on top.

Food is emotional for us. We have good and bad memories around food. So, it's a choice each and every time we eat as to what kind of experience we will have. Do I like spaghetti and ice cream because of my great memories of my dad? Yes! Do I also like them because they are generally good? Probably. The point is that I can make a choice between just eating, enjoying what I'm eating, and (even more so) having a great experience while I'm eating. It's totally up to me.

As a self-appointed *Qualitarian*, I choose the latter. I choose to enjoy eating and dining and cooking—all of it—even if it's just a scoop of peanut butter on a spoon or a roll of sushi at a Japanese restaurant.

I heard of a study where tourists who sat and dined for hours with some great friends in an outdoor café in Spain thoroughly enjoyed the taste of the wine they were drinking. They liked the wine so much that they shipped some home to themselves. But when drinking it later or sharing it back home with someone else, they thought the wine was sub-par. The study showed that the biochemical response to enjoying their meal so much with friends back in Spain enhanced the flavor of what they were drinking and eating.

What are you thinking and feeling when you prep food, cook food, eat food and dine out? This is a huge factor in how much you enjoy the experience. Sure, some foods just taste great. If we're in a good mood or rested or reasonably hungry, the food is going to taste even better.

I remember making a peanut butter & jelly sandwich for my daughter when she was a toddler. I found myself crying with gratitude while I was spreading the peanut on the bread. I asked myself, "Why are you crying?" Then I realized that I felt this swell of appreciation that I had money to buy groceries and a house to live in and a safe place to be. This made our sandwiches taste extra special to me.

Every time I eat white rice or drink root beer, I think about this concept of being a *Qualitarian*. Are you ready for a funny story about white rice? I grew up in the 70s in a blue-collar neighborhood. We were not rich but not poor either. We never went without food. But I was a very active athlete who was always super hungry. I couldn't wait to eat dinner every night. My mom would make a rotation of meals every week and I always enjoyed her Chinese Chop Suey with white rice and meat and vegetables. When I stayed with my dad, he always made yummy white rice from Uncle Ben's orange box.

My first husband and I grew up together in this same neighborhood. But he would always buy the cheap broken rice in the big bag from the bottom shelf at the grocery store. He didn't think it tasted different or bad—but I knew better. It actually changed the way I enjoyed a meal—or in this case: Not! I could never get past the bad rice. For me, it would just ruin my experience. Hence, my point about quality over saving a couple of pennies.

The same goes with root beer. Growing up, my mom would buy cheap root beer and cheap vanilla ice cream to make root beer floats. At the time, I thought they tasted pretty good. Then, at about 10 years old, I started earning an allowance and would buy an 8-pack glass bottle case of A&W root beer. I would lug that case home so that I could drink fancy root beer. Later, when I went off to summer camp in Mukwonago, Wisconsin, I experienced A&W root beer on tap from an official A&W stand. We'd been canoeing a mile or so across Phantom Lake to get there on a hot day. Now that root beer was delicious!

You see, It's all about the experience. When I drink root beer today, even if it's not the brand I like, I take the time and enjoy the moment—to appreciate every sip of it. This greatly increases the pleasure of each and every day. How simple is it to know that everything we eat or drink can become a source of inspiration?

This goes for something as special as a glass of water. Of course, it's important to drink the healthiest water you can access. But are you enjoying the water that you drink? Are you appreciating that you have access to clean drinking water? Are you nourishing your body with food that actually tastes good to you? These are simple yet powerful questions that many of us are not asking ourselves.

The most political thing we do each day is to eat and drink. We do it, on average, three times a day. Each time we eat, we are making an impact on the planet—good or bad. We are making an impact on our mind and heart. We are making an impact on the people around us when we eat. We all know that feeling of tasting something that was prepared with love and how good it tastes. We also know the taste of something that was prepared with very little intention or thought or love—like most fast food. It's not just about the ingredients, but about every step it took before we eat the meal.

Who doesn't love getting a massage? Very few, that's who. What if you skimp and get a quick chair massage at the airport or sit in one of those massage chairs that you can rent by the minute? Is that really the massage you want? I know I prefer the ones that last at least 90 minutes. Otherwise, what's the point? This doesn't necessarily mean that I go to a spa and pay a lot of money, although I'd never turn down a gift to go there. I seek a quality massage. So for me, that means going every week to my favorite Chinese reflexology business to enjoy 90 minutes of absolute bliss from highly expert bodyworkers. It's one of the highlights of my week. Honestly, it gives me that little something to look forward to each Friday.

The whole time I'm there, I feel this tremendous gratitude about the healing power of touch and being pampered. The practitioners do what I would call "medicinal" massage, because it hurts sometimes even when I ask for light pressure. (I'm a bit of a wimp that way. No deep tissue for me!) As a lay there, I drift off into my imagination of traveling to Asia to receive life-changing experiences that include Thai Yoga Massage and foot rubs in Cambodia and all the massage from all the places. This sincerely is one of my life goals: traveling the world, visiting great museums, eating fantastic food, and getting magnificent massages.

Coaching Tip:

Consider that every bite you eat is meaningful. Enjoy your meals!

Qualitarian Question:

How are you feeling better, during and after eating?

2

Supreme Self-Care

Living as a *Qualitarian* can include great food and such, but let's go a step further to what I call "Supreme Self-Care." So many of us are trying to do the self-care thing, whatever that means on any given day. Most of us fail miserably. As a holistic coach trainer, I encourage my students to make sure that they're covering the basics of self-care with their clients. The main reason is that it's a lot easier to coach clients when they're hydrated, rested and moving their bodies.

The first symptom to appear when you're dehydrated is not physical. It's emotional. When you don't drink enough water, you first become irritable. Later comes the dry skin and the parched lips. Some people don't even know why they're irritated. They just are. And often it's because they simply need more water. This is such an easy fix for most of us. And it's one of those things that we know we're supposed to do. So, drinking "eight glasses" a day is a good rule. Don't worry about how big the glasses are or following some regimen that makes you feel like you have to carry a gallon around with you throughout the day. Simply start with drinking more water than you already do—unless you're one of those rare fully hydrated freaks.

Drink the best water you can find. Maybe it's alkaline water or carbon-filtered water or—better yet—actual spring water. Drink out of glass containers like Lifefactory® bottles or stainless-steel bottles, since drinking out of plastic bottles is less safe. When you're on the run and need to grab something at a convenience store on a road trip—or prefer purchasing large plastic containers of water—be sure to purchase "spring water" instead of "drinking water" because it comes initially from a natural spring whereas the latter basically comes from a tap. These seemingly small choices can make all the difference in your overall health.

Next we move from hydration to movement. The first symptom that shows up from living a sedentary lifestyle is mild depression. Later comes the fatigue and stiffness. So move your body every day. This is vital to your well-being. It doesn't even matter much how you moved it.

If you were to pick just one way to move your body each day, be sure to move your spine. When you move the synovial fluid that lives in your vertebrae, your brain thinks, "I'm alive!" There are three main ways to move your spine, so spend maybe 10 minutes each day loosening up this fluid along with your joints and muscles. The first way is like wringing out a rag—gentle twists like Tai Chi where you stand with your feet approximately hip-distance apart and then go from side-to-side while dangling your arms to each side you're twisting. Another way is undulation forward and back like how a cat arches her back up or how a dog arches his back downward. The third way is over to the side like you're leaning over to make a crescent half-moon shape.

The key is to not combine any of these movements. Reaching down to a low drawer to pull something out of it like a purse while twisting both to the side and down can cause damage. This can hurt your lower back in a micro-sense, where you don't feel it right away but can affect you long-term. Have you ever been in the front seat of a car and reached for something heavy in the back seat and regretted it later? This is why.

Of course, healthy movement means little if you're not well rested. The first symptom that shows up when you're unrested is agitation. Later comes tiredness and lack of focus along with many other unhealthy symptoms. Lack of sleep or rest can lead you to a road-rage moment.

Humans are perfectly designed for sleep. We are dual-hemispheric sleepers—meaning that both sides of our brains sleep at the same time. This is different from cats, cows and sharks, who are unihemispheric sleepers. They sleep with only one side of their brains at a time. This is why a sleeping cat opens one eye when you walk into a room. The other side of her brain is asleep. This allows them to be safe in their environment by being ready for whatever or whoever enters the room. This also allows cows to sleep upright and sharks to keep moving in the water as they sleep.

There's nothing like a great night's sleep! You wake up feeling not only phys-ically rested but mentally clear and emotionally grounded. That expression of 'needing to sleep on it' rings true, since we often wake up with a fresh perspective on how to handle something or feeling more confident about a decision we need to make. It also levels us out emotionally in terms of our relationships, especially with the person who may be sleeping next to us.

It's such a great feeling. But many of us are only experiencing this rarely—maybe on vacation or on a weekend. Our bodies are well designed to get about 10 hours of sleep each night—the time between the sun going down and its rising the next morning. In the 1950s, North Americans were, on average, getting about 10 hours of sleep per night. That number has been cut almost in half—in just seven decades. And we wonder where 'road rage' came from. Evolutionarily, humans can't possibly catch up to the biological and physiological changes caused by nearly halving the amount of sleep we used to get when we were living more on a harvest schedule.

As a holistic coach, my clients ask me how much sleep they should be getting. This is different for each person depending on their Ayurvedic dosha or their current circadian rhythm or their natural disposition. Here's an easy way to find out how much you personally need. For three days in a row, don't set an alarm. Go to sleep when you're tired and make sure you're sleeping in a totally dark, cool room with circulating air. You want to replicate a cave that is damp, cold and dark. Remember, we came from caves and this is a more natural environment for the way we naturally sleep.

Dark—as in black-out curtains dark—like a cave. No night lights and preferably no electronics plugged in. Electronic magnetic fields (EMFs) emitting from any machine can keep the brain awake. So unplug your lamps instead of just turning them off. A plug in a socket emits more EMFs than if the lamp isn't plugged in.

Cool—as in cold. About 65 degrees Fahrenheit—like a cave. This has many health benefits including fat-burning and full REM sleep.

Damp—as in high humidity—like a cave. If you live in a dry climate, get yourself a humidifier.

Circulating air—as in a ceiling fan, box fan or fresh air from a window. This replicates the natural element of wind.

On the third morning when you awake, note the hours you slept. That gives you an indicator of the amount of sleep you currently need. This changes throughout your life because of hormonal responses. Children, especially teenagers, do not get lots of sleep because of their development phases. As we age, our need or desire for sleep changes.

"But my cell phone is my alarm!" That's how most of my clients respond. HeartMathing research shows that there's an electro-magnetic field emanating from your heart that is 60 times stronger than the electrical activity generated by the brain. This energy can be measured several feet in all directions. Crazy, huh? What might be the reason that our heart can pulse out an electric current so strong that it may communicate our emotional state to others nearby? There are theories—but who knows?

Either way, it's an interesting concept to think about how we typically hold our cell phones in front of our hearts when we're scrolling or texting. It's a form of interference. Our bodies are mostly water and electricity. This is why I advise my clients to put their phones in airplane mode and put them eight feet away from any part of their body to prevent this kind of mental or physical interference while they're sleeping or resting.

Artificial light (and anything electronic) creates a sense of daytime to our brains. This is why babies have trouble sleeping at night or sleeping for long periods. They have battery-powered EVERYTHING in their nurseries—mobiles above their cribs, music going to 'soothe' them, night lights—you name it. This is not a natural environment for them. So they tend to fight against it. Because electronics in their rooms give them a sense of floating around not being fully grounded, sleep experts recommend that you put a dark sheet on a crib mattress so that your baby knows which direction is "down."

When I visit Honduras, I'm always reminded of the "bat people" there. These are the ancient ancestors of the "40,000 mounds," meaning that they lived in caves many moons ago. They, like the farmers and other live-by-the-rules-of-nature folks, know the power of fully resting for long periods.

Some of us don't need a full-night's sleep but benefit from napping or daytime resting breaks. Power naps and sleeping pods have become popular for a reason. Many of us are so tired during the day that we need a quick recharge. Here's a tip on how best to "power nap." Tesla and Einstein used to do this. Put your head down on your arms leaning forward on a table or desk—for only 10 minutes. You want your brain to be prone, because when your brain floats in your skull horizontally, your brain thinks you're fully asleep—even if your eyes are open. So, it doesn't work as well if you're trying to catch a quick upright nap sitting in your car, because there your brain is floating vertically in your skull. Because of gravitational pull, this replicates you being awake.

The same goes for lying down. This is a better way to replicate sleep, but harder to get up after only 10 minutes. Research shows that a 10-minute prone nap can easily replicate an hour of sleep at night. If you missed two hours last night, you can take two 10-minute power naps throughout your day to get the rest you need. Keep in mind: it's not a 20-minute nap, but two 10-minute naps because a 20-minute rest can make you feel groggy.

The beauty of focusing on your hydration, movement and rest is that they work in combination with each other. When you get a good night's sleep, you have more energy to exercise or move your body throughout the day. When you move your body, you are more tired when heading to bed. When you drink enough water throughout the day, you have more hydration to help with physical energy to exercise. When you move your body more often, you get thirsty— especially for water. The three work hand-in-hand.

"How many glasses of water should I drink?" I hear this question often. "How much time should I spend exercising?" is another one. I recommend the power of using the number eight. Start with eight glasses of water a day, eight hours of sleep each night and maybe eight minutes of moving your body.

Your body knows what it needs. Trust it. Your body holds information that you can rely on to move you in the direction of enhanced health. These *Qualitarian* practices are both the easiest and hardest things you'll ever do.

They are easy because they are simple to implement. They are difficult because you will go through what I call a "Healthy Habits Rebellion." You will resist some of these easy-yet-challenging steps.

First of all, we resist the word "healthy" because it's yet another reminder that we're not doing what we know is best for us. I don't even like the word "healthy"—haha—or even more so, "healthfully." I've always disliked these words.

I used to work for *Vegetarian Times* magazine. It was an incredible experience to work there, but I must admit that the words, healthy, healthfully and healthily came up quite a bit in my writing and editing. Ugh—we need new words for these concepts!

I have a professional coach colleague, Tash Weddle, who says that she witnesses people changing bad habits for only one of two reasons. People either get sick and tired of being sick and tired—or they start doing something that feels really good and they want more of that good feeling.

Her clients, who typically spend a few months with her learning how to eat better and move more, usually go through a Healthy Habit Rebellion within the first week due to resisting the change to their routine.

Do they feel better when they get a good night's sleep? Yes! Do they feel better when they eat healthier foods? Yes! Do they feel better after stretching and exercising with her? Yes!

Then why do they stall or stop along the way? Another professional coach colleague and I were chatting the other day about change. She mentioned that she despised change. I asked her whether that might be a conditioned response.

We are all different when it comes to what we like or dislike. But sometimes I wonder whether we "hate change" because we're taught to hate it. What if change was the best thing for us? What if changing our routine or sleep schedule or diet is the key to changing everything for the better.

Qualitarians thrive on quality systems and quality practices. What system or practice are you inspired to improve today?

Coaching Tip:

Try getting one extra hour of sleep to see how it feels. Try drinking one more glass of water throughout the day. Try moving your body an additional five minutes today to see what difference it makes for you.

Qualitarian Question:

What would it feel like if you were more rested, hydrated and active?

PART TWO:
VOCATIONAL

3

The Ethical Entrepreneur

Ever notice how you don't feel as sick on a Saturday as you do on a workday? When you're really sick, you don't even know what day it is. But when you're somewhat sick, you savor your weekends as much as possible. It's like you don't want to be sick. Rarely are children ever sick on a weekend! What if work made every day feel like a weekend? *Qualitarians* seek careers that are fulfilling and rewarding, even at certain costs.

Very few of us set out in life seeking a meaningless job or a stressful career, yet so many of us are living this reality. Maybe we venture into young adulthood with a desire to make money or to make a difference—or both. Then what we often find is a series of jobs that feel less than ideal or just plain boring.

When I went off to college seeking a dance degree, I had aspirations to someday obtain a PhD in Dance. Little did I know the obstacles that would discourage me along the way. I chose a major that inspired me and felt like me. I dreamed of a career that would take me places, including international destinations.

The quality of my choices was "high" and positive in my mind and heart. I would either do this or join the Peace Corps, since that would also fulfill my desire to travel the world and make a difference.

Then "real life" slapped me in the face. School was more than I could afford. I dropped out a couple of times. I followed a boyfriend to another state and got distracted. My hormones seemed to be more focused on my biochemistry than with the quality of my future. So many of our decisions are subtly made by the body. Our hormones are saying, "You should totally be with this person, since you could have a baby with him." Little did I realize this at the time.

I didn't have a baby with this particular boyfriend. But just shy of my bachelor's degree, I got pregnant with a different boyfriend who then became my husband. No regrets—other than this feeling like a drop in the trajectory of my upcoming career.

The quality of this new relationship became my new priority. Enjoying this romance was now my focus. I needed this pocket of time for me to give and receive love. Does this mean that I forgot about my career aspirations? Not one bit. Did this start to haunt me as the years went on? Absolutely.

The most logical choice for me, given my deep care for others, was nonprofit work. Since I love animals, I went into animal advocacy. I thrived in this environment because the quality of my experiences and the quality of my impact were aligned.

Did I make a lot of money? Nope. Did I care at the time? Not really. I was riding the wave of fulfillment. I dedicated my days to doing what felt good. I was able to take dance classes on my lunch breaks in downtown Chicago.

My "Mr. Mom" husband was home with our daughter and we barely had money to pay rent. But we were pretty happy. We decided that we wanted a quality upbringing for our daughter. No daycare for her.

They spent their days going to the park and "the folks'" house, where Grandma and Grandpa lived—her great grandmother too! They went to Cubs games in Chicago and had a blast every day. Meanwhile, I went downtown to work, enjoying my days as well.

Even though I was away from the house from 7am to 7pm (sometimes due to a long commute), I was happy with my life because quality was a priority. Quality of experiences. Quality of time spent with family. Quality over quantity. It wasn't perfect, but it was purposeful.

Years later, I realized that I was very far away from those earlier dreams. Finishing my degree became an inferiority complex, especially when I couldn't even get an interview for jobs I wanted. Without those four years of college completed I was out of the running.

Long story short: I finally figured out how to have a quality career. In case you missed it in my introduction, I'll tell it again. It happened almost by accident. After many moons of working in nonprofit jobs, a respected colleague of mine turned to me at work one day and said, "You would make an amazing life coach."

I was surprised. "Why me?" I asked. She responded, "You're so resourceful and generous—and you really care about people." Honestly, I didn't know much about the profession, which was only 25 years old at the time (back in 2005). This piqued my curiosity because I'm always looking for a quality experience.

"But I'm a terrible listener," I said. My colleague replied, "Well, that's what they teach you when you become certified." I had never heard of such a thing—a place where you can learn to be a better listener. Sign me up!

The rest, as they say, is history. I attended a school based in San Diego, California, and have never looked back. It turns out that professional coaching was my calling all along. This was due to a quality conversation with a person I valued. My soul was listening.

Does this mean that I don't regret not fully achieving my dance aspirations? Not at all. I still enjoy "dance" in various forms and will always hold a great appreciation for the art form.

After being a professional coach for seven years, I had another life-changing and career-changing conversation—this time with my current husband.

At the time I was home with our son, who was three. Because I wasn't "home" with my daughter when she was younger, I decided I wanted this quality experience with my second child.

I was chatting with my husband about whether I should return to full-time work or not. He asked me a *Qualitarian* question of sorts. He asked, "Why don't you do for yourself what you do for your coaching clients?" He mentioned how I was so successful at helping them "make money and become famous" because I was a great marketing coach.

The first thought that popped in my head was that I wanted to start a professional coach training school in Nashville, because people were always asking me about how to become a coach themselves. Then my husband said something of quality that I will never forget: "I don't think you're ever going to work for anyone else ever again."

This statement sparked something in me that I didn't even realize was there—an entrepreneurial spirit. By definition, an entrepreneur is someone who pursues a venture, typically at a financial risk. Was I ready to invest in myself this way? I guess I didn't know I was until that fateful conversation.

I decided, right there in that moment, to become an ethical entrepreneur. If I was going to be adventurous and try this out, I would do it with a quality state of mind. Based on this, I decided that I would make an impact while making an income. They would go hand-in-hand.

This quality decision set me on a trail that would forge a career path I didn't even know existed. I decided that I would start my business with no overhead and no debt. Why stress myself out doing either one of these?!

To me, being an ethical entrepreneur is about being of service first. How can I make a real difference in people's lives? This continues to drive me in my now-thriving empire I've built with love and quality actions.

Being an ethical entrepreneur also drives the way I market my business. I choose quality clients and quality team members and quality policies. When I started my business in 2012, I set out to potentially start an accredited professional coach training school with a publishing arm and accompanying events.

Because quality over all else is my way of being, I knew that I didn't want to start a school that did what others were doing. It needed to be unique and offer something cutting-edge and progressive. I wanted to equip my newly trained and certified coaches to make a true difference in the lives of their clients.

Being a *Qualitarian*, I decided that I would start a holistic coach certification. This means that my coaches (like me) would coach the whole person and respect that their clients are already whole—not missing anything they needed to become who they wanted to become.

After over 20 years in corporate and nonprofit work, I chose to create my dream job instead of trying to chase one. I remember how mad I used to get when I couldn't even get an interview for a job I wanted or wasn't chosen for a job I interviewed for since I didn't have a bachelor's degree. Now I laugh, thinking about the game I was trying to play with them.

I basically broke free from the low-quality paradigm of chasing jobs and chasing careers into a high-quality experience of making the decisions myself about my own career and my own success. I realized that I have choices!

After becoming an entrepreneur, I noticed how ingrained my thinking was about being "productive" and how I basically started replicating a corporate workday instead of listening to what my natural rhythms dictated. I would catch myself running around the house multitasking, like eating while I'm walking—without sitting down to enjoy a meal. In a sense, I think I was trying to prove to myself that I wasn't wasting time. I was going to squeeze every ounce of opportunity out of each moment. "Time is money," is part of my inner dialogue.

Managing a career at home is so different from clocking in and out at a 9-to-5 job. I laughed so hard at myself one day because I "ran" to the dog park before a podcast interview where the interviewers were going to ask me about the Law of Attraction in my life and career. I had this mentality that I didn't need to prepare for the interview because it is very easy for me to talk off the cuff about this subject. One of my dogs decided that he would play in some muddy puddles and not come when I called him, so I decided to conduct the interview from my phone in my car.

Suddenly my dog decided to bolt toward me. And out of sheer embarrassment that he was shaking dirty water over everyone, I grabbed my two large dogs and headed home. Now time was getting away from me. The podcast was set up for me to call in at an exact time after the two co-hosts had already started the show. Luckily it was audio only. But I barely made it home in time for when I was to call in. So now I'm in my driveway with muddy dogs in the back of my car hoping to do my interview well without interruption.

Then here comes Murphy's Law. My son, who was seven at the time, comes out of the front door all excited to see me. His babysitter was inside and didn't realize that I was on an important call. So she was inside the house thinking nothing of my son rushing out to greet me and the dogs.

While I'm on the live interview, my son opens the driver's side door and climbs on top of me to hug me and talk to me. I had myself on mute while the podcast co-hosts were introducing me and was panicking about how my son or dogs might add some flavor to my audio.

Shockingly, the interview went really well. And they mostly heard me talking. If only they could have seen what I looked like in my small car with my big dogs and my child in between me and the steering wheel! Talk about an entrepreneurial moment—a stay-at-home, homeschooling mom moment.

In terms of a quality vocation, nothing beats a career that you carve out for yourself—where you never have to set a morning alarm ever again. This is something I highly prize about my business. I set my hours and never set them too early. My main reason for this is that I've discovered that I'm quite the night owl. I am creative in the evenings—and entrepreneurship is a highly creative field. My circadian rhythm is now better set for what my body needs.

Luckily, my son sleeps as much as I do—and we're on the same circadian rhythm of sorts. We both go to bed around midnight and get at least 10 hours of sleep. Sometimes I'll get up before him and get some work done, which is a nice bonus. I no longer dread mornings—mostly because I'm not awake for them!

Coaching Tip:

Consider the benefits and challenges of becoming an entrepreneur.

Qualitarian Question:

Are you cut out to become an entrepreneur?

22

Coaching Tip:

Consider the benefits and challenges of becoming an entrepreneur.

Qualitarian Question:

Are you cut out to become an entrepreneur?

22

4

Every Day Feels Like Saturday

Every day feels like Saturday to me. You know, that feeling of, "Oh, I get to do whatever I want, and I don't have to go to work tomorrow and the whole day is ahead of me," feeling. I pride myself on this new normal for me.

After nearly 10 years in business, I have finally perfected the art of the 3-day workweek. This is a concept that my colleague, Antoinette Placides, coined. As an entrepreneur coach, she helps her clients have long weekends for family and fun with only a Tuesday-Thursday "workweek."

After trying it this way for a while, I finally landed on a Monday-Wednesday-Friday schedule for my three work days. On these days I take appointments and train my holistic coach students. I leave Tuesdays and Thursdays open for "whatever the heck I want to do" days.

This freedom is so liberating! I have lunch with my twin sister. I might get a massage. I sometimes go watch a double feature at a local indy film house. I might run errands just for the heck of it and take my sweet time doing them. I go to the park with my dogs. I go to yoga class. I volunteer. I write. I watch tv. I play. I love these days because I decide how my time is spent—no one else.

I remember so vividly when my husband prompted me about doing my own thing. That same day I wrote down a description of a "perfect weekday." It included having lunch with a friend, going to yoga class, dropping off my son at school after walking through our neighborhood to get there. It also included working—but in a way that was more organic.

Years later, I realized that I was living that description. Gone were the days when I had to run errands on my lunch hour that nearly evaporated before my eyes. Gone were the days of giving all of my energy to my employer.

Living a *Qualitiarian* lifestyle is so much about energy management. Where do you choose your energy to go? Whom do you choose to give it to? "My time is my own," starts becoming, "My energy is my own." Life starts feeling like a series of choices instead of a series of mandates.

As a professional coach, I notice that my clients fall into one of two categories. Some are the, "I wonder what's going to happen today," types. The others are the, "I decide what happens," types. Neither is good nor bad, but they are certainly two very different ways of being.

The "wondering" ones are waiting to see what circumstances brings—what others do—what others request of their time and energy. The deciders are more proactive and more assertive about how things go down. They are better at saying, "no," to things at first glance since they are mindful about how saying, "yes," may affect their day.

Ask yourself right now, "How much of your day is spent catering to others and waiting around for something?" Then ask yourself, "What would you like to do with this extra time if you started saying 'no' and stopped waiting?"

Many of us live in the "if only I had time" paradigm. I wish I had time for this or that. If only I had time for fun hobbies or more time with family and friends. I wish I had more time to take longer vacations—more time for what I really want to do. But this is an illusion. Most of us never get to that place of finding the time.

Sometimes this is about being specific regarding what we mean by "time." I had a client once who talked a lot about how she never had time for herself. She cared for her aging mother who lived with her and also had young children. She was of the "sandwich generation," where she was the bologna in between two pieces of bread—a different generation on either side.

I asked her what she would do with this "time" she craved. She immediately responded, "I would read." So I asked her what she would read. "I have about a half dozen books in my bedroom that I would love to read someday."

(Many of my clients live in that "someday."

"Someday, I'll travel the world."

"Someday, I'll get a college degree."

"Someday, I'll run a marathon.")

I asked this client, "How much time each day would you like to devote to reading?" She thought and thought, smiled and finally answered, "Fifteen minutes." This surprised me. I love it when my clients surprise me. I thought she might answer with, "At least an hour," or something like that.

Then I asked, "Where would you like to do this daily reading?" "On my bench in my bay window in my bedroom." So, I followed up, "What's on this bench right now?" "Lots of sewing projects." So, I kept going. "When would you like to clear off that bench?" She answered with excitement, "Today!"

"Great. When would you like to start your 15 minutes of daily reading?" "Monday." (This was a Saturday.) "What time of day will you do this?" Now she stalled a bit. This is where she struggled trying to accomplish this simple thing for herself amongst all the goings on of daily life as a caregiver, mother, wife and daughter.

After a pause, she answered, "On weekdays between 11:45am-noon since that's when I'm not technically doing anything. That's the time of day while my mom and I are waiting for her transport to her day visits to assisted living."

Then I asked her a final question. "What is it going to mean to you to carve out those 15 minutes each day to read from one of those books?" She looked at me like she was surprised that she figured out how to make this happen after so many years of dust building up on the books that she longed to read in her bedroom. She started to cry. For her, the quality of her day would improve tremendously, simply by taking 15 minutes to do something enjoyable—something just for her.

Ask yourself right now, "What can I do—even if it's just for 15 minutes or 15 minutes daily—that would greatly improve the quality of my life?" Now ask yourself, "What time of day will I do this?" This simple practice will bring powerful results to your life and your daily routine. Our lives are a series of events—a series of moments—a series of 15-minute intervals.

Think for a moment about special memories you hold. Maybe it was a first kiss—maybe a meaningful conversation—maybe a feat of some kind. This likely happened within a 15-minute period. Our most precious moments in life are fleeting. Choosing these moments is possible. Choosing 15-minute experiences is very manageable.

The next time you think something is hard or nearly impossible, spend 15 minutes doing it or planning it or imagining it or even just taking one step in that direction. You might be amazed at what happens.

One thing that might happen is that you keep going after 15 minutes. Let's say your overwhelming task is decluttering. Spending 15 minutes cleaning out a junk drawer or closet feels really good—and very likely will lead to more productive minutes. Taking a 15-minute walk feels great—so great that you might want to keep walking. This is more manageable than the thought of "exercising each day." Frankly, that seems boring. But a 15-minute anything seems easy.

Coaching Tip:

Set aside 15 minutes for yourself today to do ANYTHING you'd like.

Qualitarian Question:

What do you offer the world in terms of your career?

PART THREE:
SOCIAL

5

Chasing People

I used to chase people like I used to chase jobs. I got to a good point in my career where I started deciding where I wanted to work, then pursuing that employer. Sometimes I started as a volunteer at a nonprofit or an intern to get my foot in the door, knowing that they would fall in love with me and offer me a paying position.

One of my greatest weaknesses is chasing people and emotionally bull-dozing them. I'm a Taurus, so I naturally have this bust-through-a-brick-wall energy. I have been told on occasion that my emotional expressions are too much. I have marinated people in love and have thrown a tsunami of love at them—sometimes without their consent.

Ask yourself, "What are the quality relationships in my life right now?"

Many of us have heard about surrounding ourselves with people we emulate and that we are the sum of those around us. This can be a challenging feat to find these folks, or a realization that the people around you are not the people you want around you. The company we keep is important. And the company we seek is likely telling us who we'd rather be or how we'd rather be.

It's easy to say that we can benefit from finding quality people to work alongside or have friendships with. But it's not always easy to know who they are or how to attract them into our everyday lives.

I have found that people (like jobs) are easier to access than you think. They're just people. Maybe you admire a writer or blogger. Maybe you think that this person wouldn't necessarily want to be your friend or colleague. Or…maybe they might.

Most of us live in a, "They would never want to be my friend," paradigm. Have you ever reached out to your favorite author or songwriter or speaker or podcaster about what their work means to you? It's easier than ever to do this since we live in an instant-message-away world. This doesn't mean that Brené Brown will immediately message you back, wanting to be your best friend But amazing things can happen when you find the courage to reach out to people.

There's a reason that you like or love certain people. They represent qualities or values that resonate with you. They are attractive for a very specific reason. They are you. They are reflecting back to you qualities within yourself you'd like to maybe activate or express.

Your desires are not random. They are calling you to learn something from someone or to grow emotionally or otherwise. There's a reason that not everyone is attracted to everyone. Nature has a way of balancing things out.

For example, we don't all have the same type when it comes to physical attraction. I can recognize if someone is handsome, but they might not be my type. There's a difference. And that difference lies within you.

Maybe biochemistry is calling your hormones to "make a baby" with someone, since our species is always in survival mode. Maybe your heart is unhealed and you're calling someone in to help heal that hurt. Maybe you recognize a similarity, and it helps you feel less alone.

I spent way too many years chasing love and attention from others. It was a huge mystery—that I could care so deeply about someone, yet that certain someone didn't reciprocate deep emotions.

Two things helped me realize what I was doing and why I was doing it. First, I was trying to fill an empty hole of longing for someone to genuinely love me. Second, I was mending my mostly broken heart from my childhood and from familial cellular emotional pain.

My father was orphaned at ten years old. He had already lost his mother at age three and his sister at age eight. I inherited some of this brokenheartedness. My namesake, Desirée, is the aunt I never met whom my father adored.

It's a cellular signature of sorts. When my dad went to an orphanage in Chicago, he had a small box of photos and mementos from his family. There were only a few of his father, sister and ancestors—just one photograph of his mother, who died from breast cancer. He doesn't remember her except for a vague memory of her apron strings.

Being named after my aunt feels so special. I'm an identical twin, and I received her name since I was the first one out—eight minutes before my sister. My dad told me stories about his beautiful sister who was a dancer and named after Napoleon's mistress and "true love." There was a hefty handful of emotional messaging right there!

In a way there's always been a longing of sorts in my soul. I tend to romanticize love, including unrequited love—like the legend of Napoleon being in love with Desirée but discarding her. Either way, I fully stepped into this role. And in some odd ways, have fulfilled part of my destiny in doing so.

Here's the important realization along the way: I can continue living out the pain of my family's past, or I can make another choice. I can choose to love "love" when it's healthy. I can make a choice in my favor. I don't always do this, but I've learned that these choices are available to me.

Are you choosing to love those who are less interested in your love? Are you, like an octopus, reaching out your tentacles to kidnap, then yank people toward you? Are you welcoming people or bothering people?

I have learned to "be the metal—not the magnet." This has taken me decades to semi-accomplish. Instead of being the magnet that is trying to vacuum in the attention of others, I become the material that others are trying to attract.

I do this in my personal life and my professional life. As a business owner, I have learned the subtle marketing strategy of being the metal versus the magnet. Most folks are doing magnetic-marketing or attraction-marketing—ugh! Lots of businesses are funneling folks into their programs and services. No one likes to be funneled.

If you're an entrepreneur or corporate employee, you are likely trying to draw in people to purchase something or to have things go well for you in meetings or negotiations. Are you feeling desperate about this? Do you feel nervous if certain people don't like you or don't want to do business with you?

If so—stop. This will get you nowhere. Instead, try being the person that they can't wait to hear from or wait to get attention from. This is energetic. This requires the kind of confidence that you may not currently hold. Try it anyway.

Whenever you find yourself wanting or wishing or hoping or dreaming about a relationship you seek, shift that energy into a claiming and requesting mode. As Jim Carrey says, "Hope is a beggar."

Coaching Tip:

Imagine in detail your next ideal friend, partner, child, or colleague.

Qualitarian Question:

Are you the person you need to be for your next great relationship?

6

Marinating Children in Love

This works with parenting too. You can actually call into being the kids you want. If you're already a parent, ask yourself if you wished for those children before they arrived. Most likely, you did. What else can you wish for?

I have a close friend, Sara, who always tells her two boys (who are now adults) that she wished for them before they were even born. Imagine the love those two boys must feel when they hear this! *Qualitarians* feed off of tremendous positivity that is inherently abundant. It's actually very hard to be negative, although some people seem to have perfected it!

Children are born positive. Typically they are smiling and laughing and seeing the beauty of the world. As adults, we have to remind ourselves that this world is a safe and positive place for us. If you, as a child, were not marinated in love—you basically grew up with low-quality fertilizer. It's like you are a cake being baked with cheap ingredients. It's still a cake and might, from the outside, look like an edible cake. But when someone bites into it, it leaves them longing for something more delicious.

Are you the kind of diner in a restaurant who feels disappointed if the food is just okay? I am. Not all of us are foodies but having an average-tasting meal is a letdown. It's a missed opportunity for me.

When I was growing up, I only remember seeing my grandparents a few times of the year for holidays, when my grandmothers would cook elaborate meals. The pies, turkeys and sides were beautiful to look at, but sometimes the food tasted off.

This might be, in part, because one of my grandmothers was always angry. She was stressed and frustrated, scuffing her house slippers across the kitchen floor. She glared at my grandfather from across the dining room table with such contempt! Perhaps it was because he was such a happy-go-lucky kind of a guy. Who knows? Their life, not mine.

I remember enjoying these meals but there was also an underlying stress for me. Were these meals made with love? I want to assume yes, but sometimes I wonder if the intent to be loving was somehow the missing ingredient?

Speaking of marinating, I remember my daughter's friends being surprised that I cooked dinners for my daughter instead of getting takeout or picking up fast food. Aubrey's favorite meal was salmon with asparagus. When her friends came over for dinner or stayed overnight, they were shocked that I made meals from scratch. They were perplexed with fresh asparagus instead of the canned version.

My son enjoys baking together in the kitchen. He enjoys it when I cut up his strawberries for him. He is delighted when I make him pancakes in the morning that aren't microwaved. No judgment, by the way, if you do things differently. This is simply an element of my parenting.

Are you preparing meals for your kids or maybe with them? Maybe you're taking them out for special meals. Maybe you're allowing them to choose what takeout meals you eat. Maybe you eat around a dining table WITHOUT your phones!

If you're a parent, do you marinate your kids with love? If so, how does that affect them? If not, how might that affect them? As a child, I was not marinated in love. I think this is the main reason I seek love as an adult.

Do your kids know that you love them? If so, HOW do they know? Every child is different. So do you make the effort to meet them in their own special way? How would you like to marinate your children in love?

Coaching Tip:

If you're a parent, you can remind your child what they mean to you.

Qualitarian Question:

What kind of parenting is possible for you?

7

Social Media Symphony

Social media is a big stew for all of this. People are eager to meet each other, catch up with each other, find each other, uplift each other and sometimes devour each other. What a magnificent social experiment it has been!

Scrolling on social media can be an emotional roller coaster and biochemical stew of activity. TikTok can make you laugh for hours but also make you cry with tears of compassion and sorrow.

What do you notice about yourself when you're surfing social media? Are you more comfortable creating content or consuming it? Are you judging others or yourself? Are you enjoying it or feeling stressed as a result?

As humans, we hold a negative bias, so it's natural for us to be a bit dismissive or critical of others. But is it more than that for you? Dr. Sister Jenna expertly shares that humans would be a whole lot better off if they stop doing three things: 1) Criticizing, 2) Complaining, and 3) Comparing.

Are you criticizing others on social media, even if it's just in your head? Are you complaining about how others do things on social media or what they're saying or how they're saying it? Are you comparing yourself to others, feeling less-than or more-than?

I try to conduct a social media symphony of my own. Facebook can feel like a feeding frenzy or a friendly playground. Twitter trolls thrive in a toxic environment of insults and knee-jerk responses. Instagram's images can both inspire us and create insecurity, since we tend to compare ourselves to others and their illusory posts. YouTube can feel like a rabbit hole of discovery or it can become numbing, aimless wandering.

"Nice to e-meet you," has become a norm where we get to decide ahead of time if we might like someone or not—simply based on their online presence.

We scan their posts to determine whether they belong in the "I want to be this person's friend," or, "Who does this person think she is?"

Qualitarians are focused on the quality of their time on social media and their interactions online. This doesn't mean that more time online is worse than less. This is for each of us to decide for ourselves. How we spend our time is telling. Are we energized or drained after being on social media? Are we stressed or relaxed?

If you create content, are you nervous about being fully yourself? Are you hoping people will "like" or "love" your posts before you even create the posts? Are you hoping or dreading to go viral?

Think about the people you enjoy most on social media. Do you like it when creators make you laugh? Do you enjoy everyday people just being themselves? Do you like learning from others? Do you savor the variety of people and experiences you're watching?

Socially, one of three things typically happens when we meet someone new, whether it's in person or online. We might think they're cool and want to hang with them. We might utterly dislike them for no good reason. We might feel indifferent.

These three categories are leading us. Our instinct is basically telling us that the "cool" folks are the ones who we might benefit from or learn something from. The "ew" folks are also telling us a lesson—probably not to go there. The indifferent ones are most likely the ones to steer clear of, since our intuition is telling us that there's not much to see here.

Coaching Tip:

When you spend time on social media, lean into being positive.

Qualitarian Question:

What are you thinking and feeling when you hit that "post" button on social media?

8

Giving + Receiving

Part of living a *Qualitarian* lifestyle is learning how to give and receive well. Ask yourself right now: "Do you prefer giving or receiving?" There's no need to ask why. Just observe your answer for now. Do you like to give gifts? If so, what do you like about it? Do you like to send a loving message in a letter to a loved one? Do you enjoy being on the giving side of things?

Or do you prefer being the recipient? Neither is good nor bad. But this awareness helps us live our lives more powerfully. If you love receiving gifts, what's your favorite part? Is it that someone is being thoughtful—no matter what the gift? Is it that specific gifts speak to you?

One of the most interesting things about humans is that we have these preferences but don't always act on them. For example, have you gifted someone lately if you like gifting people? Have you been clear about asking for gifts if that's what you like?

The idea of something is sometimes stronger than the action of it. We miss friends but don't make the time to call them or write to them or meet up in person. We think and feel about them, but they don't even know it. We get busy with life. We put things off like sending someone a care package or a postcard. We put off making lunch plans with those who we miss. Time goes by. Life rushes by.

A *Qualitarian* takes time for people, even when life feels too busy. A *Qualitarian* realizes and acts upon these important relationships. If we all had a dime for every time someone said they were "too busy" to do something—ugh— we'd all be billionaires!

Whether you prefer to give or receive, keep in mind that many times, gifts come in the form of non-materials. A phone call, a prayer, a gesture, a reach-out. These are all so meaningful. We all have our favorite people who we yearn to spend more time with—maybe an old friend from college or a neighbor we rush back to when coming home from work. Maybe it's a grandparent who could really use a postcard or visit. Maybe it's someone who doesn't know how much you care.

I remember so vividly a letter I wrote to my gymnastics coach. It was many years after I spent every week with her at our local gymnasium. She was my second mom and my favorite person in the whole world. She was my saving grace.

Debbie came into my life when I was eight years old. Thanks to my mom, who started teaching my twin sister and I at age three, I already thought of myself as a gymnast. I also took dance classes, which only enhanced what I did as a gymnast.

Debbie was a beautiful, young blonde woman who held such power that I was in awe of her. She was funny and spunky and direct and confident. She was loud in a good way and always stood up to men, which both surprised me and delighted me.

Six years of my life were spent under her guidance and encouragement. I looked forward to each and every time with her in the gym. I enjoyed the trampoline, vaulting, tumbling, uneven parallel bars, and balance beam (my favorite). She played loud music in the gym that included Donna Summer, Barbra Streisand and Blondie—more empowering women. My time with her was filled with laughter and hard work.

She was my biggest cheerleader—not just at gymnastics competitions but in life! Even if I fell off the beam, she always lifted my spirits with her incredible down-to-earth positivity. After moving to a different part of the state, I still went to visit her—and even took my daughter to meet her.

Then one day, I sat down to write a letter to her—one of those you-changed-my-life letters. I wrote about what she meant to me and how she kept me going at times in my childhood when I felt like giving up. I applaud her for standing up to my stepfather, who was a scary dude. This meant absolutely everything to me.

Did it matter if I actually mailed the letter? Maybe not. But she lit up like the Fourth of July when she received it. She was surprised at the deep level that she mattered to me. She was surprised that she was such a force of nature in my childhood. She cried because she didn't know about some of the things I was going through, though she had her suspicions.

I still have a copy of this letter today. It means that much to me that I wrote it and that I shared it with her. One letter! Imagine someone in the future finding this letter in a storage box who doesn't know me or Debbie. Imagine them reading these thankful words to a mentor. Or imagine this letter getting tossed out with some garbage after Debbie and I are well and gone.

The energy inside that letter lives forever. No matter who reads it or not, it contains my appreciation for Coach Debbie and for the many days we spent together. Now think about someone in your life who could use a letter like that. Have you reached out to someone from your childhood who meant a lot to you or who did something significant for you? What might happen if you did?

Imagine you receiving a letter like that—or a phone call or a visit. What an incredible gift that would be! We have so many choices these days. We can record a video or video-chat with someone. We can send them a letter or package. We can email or text them. We can visit them.

A couple of years back, I was visiting my mom in Wisconsin and had the thought of visiting other friends there who lived a couple of hours away. My intention was to take a day or two out of a week's trip to drive a couple of hours to one friend, then a couple of hours to another friend, then a couple of hours back to my mom's—potentially spending the night in one of the two other cities.

Time got away from me and I said to myself and my friends, "I'll come on my next visit." One of those friends was in battle with cancer. She passed away before I got back to Wisconsin. How easy it was for me to say, "next time." I deeply regret not visiting her. I deeply regret not taking this seriously. Part of me thought that it wasn't urgent. After she died, another part of me realized how foolish that was.

The last time I saw her in person (in a different state) was the day she told me about her first cancer diagnosis. She and I worked together many moons ago, and she was such a pivotal person in my life and in my career.

Carrie was a very bright light in my life. She shined like no one else I had ever met. Her bright blue eyes sparkled and her smile lit up every room. Her laugh was contagious, and she was truly someone who made me feel amazing when I was around her. Did I share this with her while she was alive? Yes. Did she know I loved her? Yes. Did she get a card from me shortly before her passing? Yes. Do I still talk to her? Yes.

The *Qualitarian* in me regrets not making that couple-of-hours drive to visit her. I can rationalize all I want. But the truth of the matter is, I felt drawn to going and I didn't. I said "No" to the idea. I said "No" to her. I said "No" to myself. This lesson lives with me now.

Please make the effort to reach out to those you love. Please give them attention and love and gratitude. There's nothing more important than our relationships to ourselves and those we love. There's no other point of existence without fellow humans.

You can even give those who don't know you—like writing a letter to a chaplain at a prison, asking them to give a note to someone who doesn't receive mail. You can write to someone at a military base overseas, again by writing to the chaplain, asking them to pass along a letter to someone who doesn't receive personal mail. You can rock babies at your local hospital, the ones who are orphaned or the ones who need extra bonding when parents can't be in the NICU around the clock. There are actual programs for this, like reading to children in hospitals and spending time with seniors in homes.

You may or may not be drawn to doing this, but if you are—please do. Volunteer in your community or online for a charity of your choosing. Reach out to old friends and make new ones. Even if it's not in person, you can make a world of difference for someone just by one gesture.

My best friend passed away when we were thirty. I remember receiving a letter from his mother. She mailed me a card and a photo of her son's son, the only thing we really had left of him. My friend's son was born only days after his passing, and he never met his dad due to unusual circumstances around his death.

The letter arrived on a day when I really needed it. I was coming home from a long day at work. I missed my friend so much, and this letter and photograph brought me to my knees. It was painful and beautiful at exactly the same time because my friend's son looks just like him. It made me miss him more and miss him less, all at once.

My friend's mom probably didn't realize how much this letter would mean to me. It means even more now, since she has passed herself. We really don't have much time with each other, do we? Life and time move by both slowly and suddenly. I have learned to act when I get that impulse—to have a meal with a friend or to send someone a care package. It's not enough to think about doing it and having the best of intentions.

I challenge you today: Write a letter to someone, knowing that it might brighten their day. Maybe it's a child you know. How fun is it when a child gets a letter in the mail? So fun. Maybe it's a family member who hasn't heard from you in a long while. Maybe it's a friend from childhood. Maybe it's a former coworker. Send them something. Find their address and have some cards and stamps handy. Do this once a month. Do it for them.

Coaching Tip:
Give fully and receive even more fully.

Qualitarian Question:
Are you receiving as well as you are giving?

9

The Corrector

One aspect of living a *Qualitarian* lifestyle is to acknowledge the parts of yourself that need mending. If we aren't here to heal each other, what are we here for? I'm not one to look for flaws within myself or others because I believe that criticism is wasted energy. But I've noticed something repeating itself within me that I call being a "corrector."

Ask yourself right now: "What would you identify as your main flaw?" I'm not talking about what a book or methodology would call it. What would *you* call it? For me, being a corrector is a constant nuisance, not only to me but to all those around me who experience it. I correct people's grammar, but not because I truly care—it's more that I can't help myself. It's a compulsion.

Is this a quality experience? No! Is this super annoying to those who I correct? Yes! Have I been able to stop myself after decades of doing it? Unfortunately, no. My point here is to notice. Notice what you're noticing about your life—about your behavior. Observe how it makes you feel. Observe what you're observing in others when you flex the muscle of your main flaw.

The reason I'm asking you to home in on your main flaw is that many of the smaller ones will fall away if you focus on the big one. Many of us go to therapy or go round-and-round in our heads with a preoccupation of noticing our little flaws.

The little ones might not seem little to others, like my according-to-me main flaw right now of being an over-corrector. You might not think that my habit of correcting people is a major thing. But trust me, it is. The worst part of it is how I correct myself and others in my head. It's exhausting.

If I focus on mending this part of me, then my other flaws or notable dysfunctions might melt away. So, what's your main flaw? When you just read that sentence, which one bubbled up first? Choose this one to mend, since your mind chose it to mend. The question is an invitation to consider some healing that may need your attention.

You don't even have to know how to mend it. Just acknowledging it is sometimes enough to heal. There's this beautiful moment of saying, "Hello. I see you. I hear you. Thank you. Goodbye."

Try this. Allow that flaw to be seen. Allow it to be fully seen. Observe it without emotion at first. The human species has an extraordinary gift of being able to observe ourselves outside of our bodies. Supposedly, we are the only species that can do this. But I'm guessing that highly sentient creatures like dolphins can probably do this and more.

Picture yourself standing in your hand. Picture this person holding an unhealed pain. Picture this pain coming from a place outside of this person. Do this without judgment. Do this with a need to understand.

Now imagine that you can do energetic emotional surgery on this person. You are able to see the flaw and heal it. You instinctively know what to do. You know exactly what to do and how to do it. There's this knowledge of how to do it.

Now imagine that you're trying to do this without being an observer. You're sitting in your feelings and thoughts. You might feel stuck or confused about what to do to feel better. You might think that there's no way out of this way of being.

A *Qualitarian* views the world as a place of possibility—a place of opportunity—a place of a million choices. So, all it takes to change something is to choose something.

For example, I can view my correcting as an annoyance or as an opportunity to learn something new about myself. I can observe the dysfunction and make a choice to change the behavior or hang on to it for dear life.

The truth is, I might not want to choose something different. Maybe I like being a corrector even though society tells me it's wrong. Maybe I'm not willing to let go of my tight rein on being right or being smart—or whatever payoff I gain from doing it repeatedly.

So, I can shift the compulsion to more of an urge. I can subtly shift into a place of acceptance and non-judgment. We've only been speaking and writing the English language for 1500 years or so. Who am I to be an expert?

It's all about choices. What choice can you make right here, right now in this very minute? We easily get overwhelmed with a sense of changing ourselves—bettering ourselves—enhancing our lives. Talk about exhausting!

As humans, we are well designed to improve ourselves and our situations. This is part of our survival instinct. We yearn to grow and learn. We become better versions of ourselves along the way. This is a natural process.

It becomes out of balance when we try too hard. When we add a hustle or a struggle into it, it starts feeling hard and uncomfortable. Ease is a natural state of being, not discomfort.

Coaching Tip:

Consider your "flaws" as a beautiful part of you.

Qualitarian Question:

Are you willing to consider that others' "flaws" are part of their beauty?

10

The Body Knows

In what areas of your life are you trying too hard? Where can you relax your grip? So many of us don't even realize how hard we are gripping. Notice how your body feels right now. Now relax your pelvis. Now relax it a bit more. Now a bit more. Even more. This moment of relaxation may help you understand how tight your muscles were gripping. Just your awareness alone is enough to change it. It's so simple to relax. Yet many of us are walking around and sitting rigid in our bodies.

Want some good news? It's super easy to relax your mind. I know, I know. Many of us experience the "monkey mind" of swirling thoughts and ideas that keep looping in our heads. The easiest way to relax your mind is to relax your body. In fact, the easiest way to do anything is to do it in the body. An example of this is someone trying to be creative. We might try to write or draw or paint or sing or dance or "be creative" and nothing comes.

When you're feeling uncreative, take a bath. Take a shower. Go for a swim. Allow the water to release your creativity. Water, by nature, is flowing. Have you noticed how creative you become after taking a shower or a swim? The body is doing the work. We get in trouble when we're trying to force the head or the heart to do something.

Speaking of the mind, a lot of people mistake this word for being about the head and your thoughts. The mind is actually composed of your thoughts, your feelings and your brain activity. So, the mind is much more complex and layered than just the head itself. This is why mindful meals, mindful walks or mindful conversations are so meaningful.

Complexity can lead to complications. Humans are very layered, so it's easy for us to get caught in the weeds of all of our thoughts and feelings. Then we impose more thoughts and feelings onto those initial thoughts and feelings. And so on, and so on.

The easiest way around this is to go to the body for peace. This is why a massage feels so good. It's not just that our muscles are getting worked, it's that our minds are relaxing as a result of our bodies relaxing. Even just the thought of getting a massage can be relaxing!

In part, this is because the brain doesn't know the difference between you experiencing something, imagining something or remembering something. If you enjoy massage, think right now about a previous massage. If you don't like massage, think about something you truly enjoy. Maybe it's eating something delicious or taking a great nap.

Your brain enjoys the experience. It doesn't matter if the experience is in the past, present or future. Thinking about a great massage on an upcoming spa day is relaxing in and of itself. Receiving a massage is relaxing. Remembering the massage is also relaxing.

Think back to a wonderful nap. My mind goes to a summer day in Iowa when I was in college. I'm not much of a nap person, but I laid down in my bed in front of an open window with a slight breeze coming in. I remember hearing a bit of noise outside, like my roommate drinking lemonade and listening to her radio. The birds were singing. As I drifted off, I remember so vividly how enjoyable it was to fall asleep like that. I remember dreaming during that nap about how great that nap was. I remember waking up and thinking how great the nap was. The whole experience was sheer pleasure.

If I need to rest my mind, all I have to do is to think about that great nap many moons ago. That's all it takes. I don't even need a nap. My brain chemistry shifts when I recall that great nap.

This is a powerful tool for manifestation. If you want to fall in love, think and feel the sensations of being in love. Imagine being in love. Remember being in love. This imagery creates an environment where being in love fully exists. You're literally creating an environment where love has to exist. Love is welcome and ever-present.

Coaching Tip:

Your brain doesn't know the difference between imagining something or experiencing something—so imagine away!

Qualitarian Question:

What are you willing to imagine for yourself?

PART FOUR:
EMOTIONAL

11

Finish Your Feelings

Aren't people so beautiful when they cry? Sure, there are a few "ugly criers" in the bunch. But for the most part, I find people most beautiful when they are about to cry, crying or lifting away from tears.

As a holistic coach trainer, I teach my students not to hand their clients a tissue when they cry during sessions. In essence, you're telling the person to stop crying. So much of our grief is a series of unfinished feelings. Interrupting someone's tears stops them in their tracks. Talking while someone is crying can also do this—so can touching them.

Have you ever wondered what might happen if you allowed yourself to fully feel your feelings? As humans, we tend to under-process emotions in the moment—when we find our feelings too intense. When we feel something painful, we back away from it.

A woman in labor knows this all too well. She might physically try to inch away from the contractions until her doula encourages her to lean into them instead. The truth is, her contraction has a beginning, middle and end—and so does everything else, including our emotions.

If you want to see an example of the opposite of this, just watch children. They feel what they're feeling. Then they let it go. They might scream and kick, but they are doing something very healthy—fully feeling their feelings. They get upset for a bit, then they're off to something else.

As adults, we tend to do the opposite. We compartmentalize our pain. We attach ourselves to feelings that eventually turn into long-standing wounds. We become the walking wounded. We save our feelings for later, sometimes much later.

Right here in this moment, conjure up an emotional pain that is currently lingering inside of you. Now ask yourself how long ago that pain felt painful.

Of course, we all experience pain in different ways and with different timelines, but many of us are hanging onto pain unnecessarily.

Your pain is your power, especially when you allow yourself to fully feel the pain and then release it. Pain is neither good nor bad, it is simply a part of our emotional wheelhouse. Pain comes first, then comes healing. If you surrender to painful thoughts and emotions, it turns out that they don't have to become your best friends.

Speaking of pain, one definition of abuse is people trying to give you their pain because they don't want to feel it themselves. Have you ever tried to dump your pain onto someone else? That impulse comes from a simple place—a discomfort. A small urge to avoid emotional pain can snowball into a larger pain that you must claim ownership of.

In this very moment, you can choose to finish a feeling. What's lingering inside of you that hasn't found its finish? What emotion can you release right now simply by deciding to nestle into the feeling in order to see it on its way? It only takes about 90 seconds or so to do this. Find the unfinished feeling, set a timer, and then feel it fully until you hear a ding. If you find yourself drifting away from the feeling, just gently go back to it. Do this until the feeling is fully finished. Notice the difference.

Of course, you might be like me who loves to hang on to feelings. I take a long bath in my feelings every day. My personality is conducive to wallowing and melancholy. My grief is like the best friend I never had. I'm actually very familiar and comfortable with pain. So I have to be careful about allowing it to become my identity.

If a counselor or coach asks me if I'm ready to release something painful, I want to say, "Yes, I'm ready." But the truth is that I cling to my pain because it's what I knew as a child. As an adult, I have had to unravel this entanglement with feeling painful emotions. As an adult, I learned that I can finish my feelings to relieve the suffering of my grief. I have said "Yes" to some of this, but I've also put some of it into the, "Soon, I'll do that," category.

I vividly remember a moment like this. My husband and I were in a hospital room after we had a late-term stillbirth. We were devastated. Both of us were emotionally exhausted and in tremendous pain. But I remember looking over at the window where he stood holding our son, saying goodbye to him.

The emotional pain was so intense that I turned away. I couldn't even bear to look at them. It's like I escaped into a world of less-than—feeling only part of the feelings. I remember feeling my husband's pain almost more than my own. After a decade of grief, I can still feel this pain. I can also release some of it—like water flowing down a stream.

After 'trying again' for a couple of years, I realized that my physical body was ready to conceive again but that my heart wasn't. On Mother's Day, I received the strangest gifts from my mother-in-law. One wrist corsage (yes, like the ones for proms) with a huge white flower represented the child we lost. A second wrist corsage with pink and blue flowers represented the twins that she wanted to "help us make via IVF" with her financial support.

As I awkwardly stood there with these two huge flower corsages, I felt extreme discomfort and a bit of anger. I walked into what was supposed to be our nursery for some future potential child we might have. I looked around and suddenly realized how everything in the room was dead. My husband's great uncle's Purple Heart and jacket from WWII. An elephant tusk carving that my husband inherited from his grandmother.

I immediately took down all the dead things and put them in a closet in another part of the house. Then I hung a cute painting of an elephant that our friend painted for our nursery. The dead elephant (tusk) was now replaced with a sweet painting for our next sweet child, regardless of the method of conception.

I decided to replace the mourning with motion. I made a quick, conscious decision to transform the sadness into hope. I emailed all my friends and asked them to see me as a healthy pregnant woman because I sensed that they were all still thinking, "Oh, that's so sad that they had a miscarriage." I swear it shifted everything.

After trying to get pregnant for over a year, we finally became pregnant (naturally!) within a few days of that super awkward Mother's Day. It was also my birthday, hence the second corsage.

Grief specialists call this grief recovery, because we can actually recover from our grief. The easiest way to do this is to finish our feelings. Have you ever been in an almost-car-accident where you think someone might hit you, but they actually don't? Then you get into a car again and still feel that anxiety. Your brain still thinks you might die.

The good news is that we can choose our emotions. We might not be able to choose our pain, but we can certainly choose what we do with our pain. If you're feeling sad, feel sad. Feel it deeply. Then make a choice to feel something else.

In professional coaching, when a client is uncomfortable with a feeling, we ask them open-ended questions like, "What would you rather feel?" Some clients get unnerved by this. The concept of choosing our emotions is foreign.

Try it right now. Center in on a current feeling. Maybe you're hungry or sad or indifferent or whatever. Allow this emotion to settle in for a moment. Now just pick another feeling. Go there. Maybe you stay there for 90 seconds or so. Then go somewhere else. It's like an internal vacation.

Feeling "negative" emotions is not your fault. But they can become your responsibility. If you've been abused, painful feelings that come from those experiences are also not your fault. What you (and you alone) decide to do with these feelings is up to you. Entirely and utterly up to you.

This is both a blessing and a curse. The good news is that discomfort can quickly subside into comfort or at least something more tolerable. The bad news is that it's your responsibility to take the next steps. This is not always easy, especially because we're not taught that this is possible.

"Let's see where this goes," is an expression that lends itself to the idea that things are not within our choosing. Try this one on instead: "You get to decide where things go. How things go. When things go. Where things go."

Yes, there are others also deciding things, so we're not necessarily in complete control. We have a symbiotic relationship with others around us. But at least we can take ownership of our own emotions. This, in turn, can form and shape our moments, our days and our lives.

Some of us wake up in the morning feeling like the day will unfold as a set of predetermined circumstances. "I wonder what's going to happen to me today?"

On the other hand, some of us wake up in the morning feeling something completely different: "I get to decide what happens to me today." Whether you believe in fate or not, this way of thinking can be very empowering, because there's a sense of personal responsibility woven inside.

Coaching Tip:

Allow grief to take its beautiful time to heal your heart.

Qualitarian Question:

What do you decide about something for yourself today?

12

Friendships

Great friends add a whole lot of quality to our lives. Great friendships are like most relationships. It takes nurturance to keep them thriving.

Life is basically a series of relationships. Friendships stand out as some of the most supportive of them. In fifth grade, I remember asking my best friend a question on her front porch that somewhat ended our friendship. I'm not even sure why I asked it. "What do you not like about me?" I don't even remember her response, but it felt like I was in slow motion when she responded. This was an incredible lesson in not "going for the negative." Wow!

Previous to that, we were inseparable. We came home to her apartment every day after school and cranked Rush's album, *2112*, in her bedroom while her brothers were cranking Black Sabbath in their bedroom. We bounced on the bed. We laughed. We made *Macaroni & Cheese*. We had sleepovers and stayed up late on New Year's Eve to listen to the radio songs of the year countdown.

In my Chicago neighborhood, we had such a vast array of ethnic groups. My best friend's name was Linda. Her parents emigrated from Poland and didn't speak English. The food in her home was stellar, especially the dumplings and desserts.

When we're in relationships, we don't think about being out of them. We have this illusion that we will have them forever. The truth is, they don't really end. Friendships live beyond the time we spend with people. Even though I'm not currently "best friends" with Linda from fifth grade, she is a permanent sweet spot in my heart.

Who pops into your mind when you think about friendships? Is this person still around? Are you in touch with them? Do they know how much they mean to you? Maybe it's time to reach out to them.

Most friendships feel effortless. Some take more effort. Are you putting quality effort into yours?

Losing friends is a sure wake-up call to understanding the great gift our friendships provide. Have you lost anyone important to you?

Remember my story about visiting my mom in Wisconsin a couple of years back? I planned to visit a friend just a couple hours away. Even though she was sick with cancer, I skipped it and convinced myself that I'd do it "next time." Unfortunately, there was no next time because she passed away before I visited Wisconsin again. We don't know when the last time is that we'll see someone. Every get-together is precious.

Carrie was not just a friend but a respected colleague. She's the one who encouraged me to become a professional life coach. If it wasn't for her, I wouldn't be writing this book.

Speaking of books, I remember her asking me about marketing. She was an exercise physiologist and we worked together at a holistic wellness center. I said, "We should open up a place called Radiant Health Institute and you can call yourself a Radiant Health educator. I made her an empty book, like a journal, and the front cover had a nice photo with "Radiant Health" on the front and her photo and bio on the back. I encouraged her to make notes about authoring a book by that title.

Years later, I was in her house and she showed me this journal on her bookshelf. She had been writing in it for years. I forgot about it until I saw it. I was so pleased that this meant something special to her, having made it to this new house of hers. I miss her and think of her often. In many ways, she's still my friend. I am grateful for her presence in my life.

Who are you grateful for? What friends of yours mean the most to you?

The best friend I ever had is also no longer alive. I met Kent the first day of college at the University of Iowa and still remember the impact of our first meeting. He was so beautiful to me. His laugh was infectious. His smile was contagious. He was so handsome! But mostly he was so intriguing to me. Kent, most definitely, was the first person I ever met who made me realize that we have past lives with people. This felt epic and timeless to me.

Before his sudden passing when we were 30, he was the person I thought about the most. We didn't always live in the same state, so there were lots of letters written and sent. This was pre-cell phone time, so our communications were more in person and over the phone. Lots of calls and lots of quality time spent together.

The memories I hold of Kent are all mine. I could write about his amazing attributes and describe him to you, but you could never know what his friendship meant to me. Grieving his loss is still an everyday occurrence for me, and he's been gone over 20 years now. One thing I don't regret is that we always told each other how much we cared, including the last time I saw him—not knowing it would be the last. He knew how much I cared.

Are you doing the same in your friendships?

Friends are so precious.

Coaching Tip:

Cherish friendships knowing that they add so much quality to your life.

Qualitarian Question:

How can you put more quality into your friendships?

13

Keeping in Touch

We all live busy lives. We all miss our friends. We all intend to spend more time with our loved ones. But we "get busy" and deprioritize it.

As a holistic coach, I've noticed that most people have around 22 people in their life who truly care for them. These circles might include family, friends and colleagues. I encourage my coaching clients to reach out to their "Top 22" monthly in order to develop and keep strong connections.

We might have a former college roommate whom we miss. We might miss a former coworker. Maybe we used to call Grandma every Sunday but now we often skip it. Maybe we yearn to reconnect with a best friend from years ago.

Some of our "Top 22" will be folks we email. Others might be a phone call, a text, a letter in the mail or an in-person visit. We generally know which medium will best communicate our reachout. Millennials often don't answer their phone or listen to a voicemail. So a text might work best for them. Grandpa might be an in-person visit. Most will be easy enough to email.

I suggest doing four things when reaching out each month. 1) Let them know what's up with you. Maybe you share a brief description of a promotion you're up for or a great restaurant you just tried. Maybe you detail a trip you took or a new book you're reading. 2) Ask them about them. If they're into gardening or crystals, ask them about it. If you know they love something in particular, ask them about it. This shows that you honor and remember who they are. 3) Let them know something you need. Maybe it's a new client for your business. Perhaps it's a recommendation for a new TV series to binge. Maybe it's a recipe for something they know how to make. 4) Ask them what they need. Maybe it's checking in on them twice a week. Perhaps it's a shoulder to cry on. Or maybe it's something you would have never considered.

Reaching out like this every month builds powerful connections. Sure, it's catching up. But it's also genuinely bonding with a simple gesture of friendship or work-related acquaintance.

But here's something to be careful about: One of my Canadian-based coach training graduates, Laura Shortridge, warns against sharing your deepest dreams with whom she calls the "dreamkillers." You know—those people in your life who don't really wish you well—the ones who relish when you fail. The fair-weathered friends and the conditional folks.

These people are not allowed on your "Top 22" list. These are the people in your life who say things like, "That'll never work," or, "Why would you major in that in college?" or, "That's not very realistic."

When you share what you need with your trusted list, they will cheer you on and support your efforts. They will send you clients and great recommendations. They care about you, so they will wish you well and expound upon your own positivity about your life and desires. They want to see you do well. You want the same for them.

Watch your own intentions as well. Remove anyone on your list if you don't truly care for them. You will not add anything to their life by reaching out with ulterior motives or insincere gestures. Be honest with yourself about equally valuable connections.

I'm a stationery nerd. I could spend hours in a stationery store. It's a lost art for sure, but I deeply enjoy finding a great store that has notecards as well as fun papers and envelopes. I like my correspondence to be unique. My mom lives in Florida where there's a *Quill & Press* retail store that's one of the highlights of my trips to visit her.

With my dear friend, Kent, whom I mentioned earlier, I would mail him letters with photos of my daughter to the point where he and his girlfriend almost felt like she was theirs based on how many photos of her were on their fridge. I sent heartfelt handwritten letters. This is quite a pastime. I also sent care packages that included fun foods and silly items like animation books and funny stickers.

I sent these packages so often that I received one back in the mail after his unexpected passing. It was so hard to open the mail knowing that he would never receive it. It included a book from one of his favorite authors and recent family photos along with a sweet note from me letting him know how much

I loved him. It's comforting to me that I was continually ever-present with my love for him. He never had to question it.

I didn't formally have a "Top 22" list back then, but he would have been at the top of it. We almost never lived in the same place, so keeping in touch through mail was fun and always a nice surprise.

Imagine the delight of a child receiving an unexpected letter from you. Maybe your niece or nephew or grandchild would love this. Maybe your child or a parent or your grandparent. Our mailboxes are full of junk mail these days, so receiving something personal is always a treat.

When I have a new student sign up for my coach training, I send them a parcel full of fun items like a YETI water bottle, a chocolate bar, maybe a candle, a crystal, a book and a handwritten note welcoming them to the Radiant family. They don't know it's coming because I use the address associated with their payment link when they sign up. I get lots of happy messages from the students after they receive their parcel.

I love sending care packages so much that I used to have a side hustle called "Personalized Parcels." I would customize shipments to customers based on someone's interests when it was their birthday or another reason to celebrate.

I know that one of the "The Five Love Languages" coined by Gary Chapman is "Receiving Gifts" but I swear mine is "Giving Gifts!" Trust me…I'm an incredible gift giver.

When I brought holiday gifts over to my friend Misti's house once, I remember saying, "This is not about you. This is about me watching you open my gift, haha."

Being a *Qualitarian* is not about buying people expensive gifts, it's about being thoughtful and timely. It's about making it special and not being predictable. Who wants boring gifts, anyway?

Coaching Tip:

Make a list of your "Top 22" and reach out to them monthly.

Qualitarian Question:

How might you affect your close contacts by frequently reaching out?

14

Face Your Fears

As a professional coach, I had a client once who came to see me with a lot of physical stress in her body. Fear manifested in her body as tension in her jaw. It was so bad that she couldn't even open her mouth fully. She was so fearful and so angry that it affected her ability to eat and speak. This is how bad it can get when you don't face your fears or fully finish your feelings.

My identical twin sister, Nese, went through something similar when we were young adults. I used to make fun of her because of the sound she would make when smoking her Virginia Slims Menthol Lights cigarettes. It was kind of a 'plucking' or popping sound when she pulled her cigarette away from her mouth.

On one of her pops, her jaw locked. She couldn't even stick a finger in between her teeth. At first we were baffled, but then it got serious. Nese went to a doctor, then to a dentist who sent her to an orthodontist. After weeks of trying to get a diagnosis, one of the physicians asked her, "Do you think this could be psychosomatic?"

"What do you mean?" she responded. He explained that it could be "in her head." Our stepmom was a social worker, so she recommended that she visit a mental health practitioner. By this time, she had lost a significant amount of weight because she could only drink her meals.

After Nese filled out all the paperwork the psychologist asked, "So, how's your life?" She explained, with a tight jaw, about how great her life was. Her boyfriend was great. Her new apartment was great. Her job was great. Her Triumph sports car was great. Her trips with her friends were great. Everything was great!

Then the psychologist asked, "Is there anything NOT great?" And after a long pause she responded, "Well, there is one thing." Every night when I go to sleep, I have a terrible nightmare. My stepfather, who's been dead for years now, is in my dream and it frightens me. He was an abusive person in my life."

The psychologist's question is one that I now consider a great coaching question: "What does he want?" Nese answered, "I don't know! I don't want to know!"

Unlike in coaching, this practitioner gave her a directive. "Tonight when you're falling asleep, I want you to turn to him and ask him what he wants." She replied, "Hell, no, I won't." This is how much it scared her.

Of course, the psychologist planted a beautiful seed with the power of suggestion. As she was falling asleep that night, she thought about what he advised her to do. In her dream, our stepfather was typically behind her in a dark corner of a room. So she started to turn to ask him what he wanted. And as she turned—poof—he disappeared.

Nese woke up the next morning with a softer jaw, although it would remain sore for many weeks. She revisited the psychologist who explained to her that facing her fears is what made him go away and release her jaw. He further explained that many of us can hold repressed anger in our temporomandibular joint at the top of our jaw.

Qualitarians are focused on fixing what doesn't work well. Mending what needs mending. Healing what needs healing, but not is a forceful way. The quality of the way we seek to heal ourselves is vital for positive growth.

Some of us prefer the band aid ripped off quickly while others prefer it pulled off very slowly. What if I gave you the choice of going away for 30 days to repair what's wrong in your life—or taking 10 years to do the same? Which one would you pick?

Neither one is right or wrong, it's just a preference. As a holistic coach, I am highly trained to respect the pace at which my clients are going. I honor the speed and the depth. Some of my clients want to 'get it over with' and others want to take their time. Both are great.

I believe that we're all here to help each other—to heal each other. When I meditate, which is rare, I receive beautiful messages about how my role in this life is to anchor consciousness. When I 'heard' this, I was relieved because previously, I thought I had to find my life's calling.

I don't regularly meditate the way others might recommend. My nervous system can't handle seated meditation as well as moving meditation. So I tend to 'meditate' more on walks and while moving. Dancing works well for me.

When I meditate, the guides that I sense describe Earth as "the planet of sorrows." They explain to me that many of us are learning how to be sad and fully feel all that is happening. They describe soul contracts so simply.

For example, if I want to learn how to forgive, then someone must harm me in order for me to forgive them. I remember saying to myself as a child, "I want to learn how to stand up for myself." So many teachers have been sent for me to learn this.

We tend to fear "bad feelings" like sadness. Yet sadness is an incredible professor of ours. If you're familiar with Enneagram work, you might not be surprised that I'm Type Four ("The Romantic") in this personality construct paradigm. This means that I can go very deep emotionally. Other types can't. That's great too, because variety is necessary. The world would be out of balance if we were all feelers or all thinkers.

Qualitarians are, at least, in touch with their feelings.

Coaching Tip:

Surrender to your inner knowledge that innately understands that fears are just as much a part of life as anything else.

Qualitarian Question:

How can you face a fear of yours without it scaring you?

PART FIVE:
MENTAL

15

What is the Mind?

You may remember that I said earlier: "the 'mind' is not just your thoughts." The mind is your thoughts, your emotions and your consciousness. It's not a body part. In other words, we don't have a mind because we are in the mind. Mindfulness is about noticing what you're noticing, observing what you're observing.

Take a moment now to try this: What are you thinking? What are you feeling? What sensations are in your body? A *Qualitarian* is someone who is aware of multiple sensations in the moment—someone who can tap into feelings, thoughts and bodily movements or tension.

Here's a great tip on being mindful and in the present moment. Lightly scratch the skin on your forearm with your fingernails. Feel this undeniable sensation that you can't NOT feel. This is the present moment. Also, slow everything down. Slow your gaze. Slow your movements. It's much easier to slow the body first, which will then slow the mind.

If you're having trouble falling asleep with lots of thoughts and emotions swirling around, becoming aware of your body can calm the mind. Think about children counting sheep. Think about putting your focus on one thing.

Eye gazing and candle gazing are great ways to become aware of your mind. You simply look at something that's not moving for a minute or more. As a holistic coach, I teach this simple technique to my clients so that they have a tool in their everyday lives to calm their mind when needed.

Choose something to look at that's below your eye level. Maybe set a timer. Look at this object. If your eyes dart away, just go back to the object. Your brain waves will begin to slow and level out. If it's a candle, the slight motion of the flame might feel comforting. You might notice your breath. You might notice the sensations of the room. The temperature. The light. The noise. This exercise gently places you into your own awareness.

Being in this "noticing place" will help you be more in the moment, more at peace, more calm. You might notice that you're not breathing. You might notice that you're sad or feeling empty. You might notice that you feel appreciation for something or someone.

You don't have to be a breathwork expert to practice mindful breathing. Something as simple as "box breathing" is a great practice. You simply close your eyes while imaging a square box in front of you. You inhale up on the left side, then exhale across the top to the right, then inhale down the right side, then exhale across the bottom to the left, then repeat.

As you practice and start mastering this, you can try stretching your square box to a rectangle and exhale on the longer sides. Exhaling is great for detoxifying your body and releasing energy. I find that inhaling is a lot easier than exhaling, which probably means that I easily absorb stuff and find it more difficult to let go of things. We are all different this way.

In everyday life, we rush around and are not very mindful. We hurry. We stress. We feel like time is slipping away. Being in a mindful state slows things down. It allows us to be in one moment at a time.

Picture yourself camping in a tent. Think of the inside of the tent as your past. Think of the outside of your tent as your future. Now imagine you opening the tent door by opening the zipper. This is the present moment.

Coaching Tip:
Try a meditation where you picture yourself camping using this imagery.

Qualitarian Question:
In what area of your life would you like to be more mindful?

16

Mental Time Travel

Humans supposedly are the only species capable of imagining ourselves in the future. This can be both a blessing and a curse.

If you are able to think of the future, you might worry about it. This is a form of anxiety. You might feel hopeful about the future but wonder if it can actually happen the way you'd like.

If you're thinking a lot about your past, you might be feeling regret. You might be feeling like you want to go back and do things differently. You might miss being younger or having a certain someone in your life.

Professional coaching focuses on the immediate, short-term future. When working with my clients, I ask questions like, "How would you like the rest of your day to go?" Because in many ways, it's up to us how we feel and what we think.

As a species, we can imagine ourselves outside of ourselves. Picture yourself standing in your hand. This is an extraordinary gift to be able to "be the observer."

Try this: Think of something that's really hard for you right now. Picture yourself sitting next to yourself and "this person" having the challenge (not you). Imagine what this person could do to solve this problem. Imagine how this person can feel differently about it. Imagine this person taking positive actions. Imagine them overcoming this hardship.

This technique can be helpful because we become objective instead of subjective. Frankly, it's hard to stay calm and neutral about a challenge because we are heightened emotionally or biochemically reacting to life.

Another way to consider this is imagining it's someone else. How can this person come to better terms regarding this challenge? How can this person feel better about this hardship? This can add an element of compassion for "this person" (and yourself!).

In my coaching, I use an exercise to imagine a scenario in which we switch lives with someone. Anyone. Pick a person and imagine living their life for the next week. Imagine you eat what they eat. You wear what they wear—think what they think. You feel what they feel. Imagine going to their job if they have one. You share a bed with their someone, or maybe they sleep alone. Imagine practicing their morning rituals. Do they have pets? What is their daily routine? What does it feel like to be in their body? What can you see when you look from their eyes? What are you sensing? What are you observing? What are you noticing?

Do you enjoy being them? Do you like their home setting? The company they keep. The sheets on their bed. The food in the fridge. Children if they're present. The shampoo in the shower. All the things.

Now, here's the fun part—or not so fun. Imagine them switching places with you for a week. Now they're going to be driving your car or shopping for your groceries and taking your walks and chatting with your friends. They'll be working at your job and feeling all of your emotions. They'll be rested or not. They'll be hungry or not. They'll be spending time with your people. They'll be smelling your surroundings and tasting your food—responding and reacting to your life.

What's your immediate thought around them living your life for a week? Do you feel bad for them? Are you excited for them? Maybe they get to have sex with your partner! Maybe they have to—haha. Do you have thoughts like wishing your bathroom was cleaner or that you have cuter underwear? Do you wish that your diet was more interesting? Are you glad that they get to pet your dogs or cats? Notice your thoughts here.

Our ability to see into our future, even for a week, is powerful and sometimes daunting.

Coaching Tip:

When thinking about your future, try to stay in the best-case scenario in your mind.

Qualitarian Question:

What's the best thing that's going to happen to you today?

17

The Flavors of Failure

Babies are only afraid of one thing. Falling. When you're holding babies a bit precariously, they sometimes jerk because they're afraid you might drop them. Babies aren't afraid of being hungry, they just get hungry. They're not afraid of getting cold, they just sometimes get cold.

What are adults afraid of? Failure.

Public speaking is often referenced as a common fear, but it's not actually the speaking itself that we are afraid of. It's not being a good speaker. Failing at speaking.

Another common fear that people claim is dying. Is it really the dying we're afraid of, or is it not living a full life before we die?

We are afraid that people won't like us back. We are afraid that we'll look like an idiot in a meeting. We are afraid of never accomplishing something meaningful.

There are lessons in failure, and they come in many different flavors. Failure may often lead to success. Everytime I fail, I ask myself, "Do I want to learn this lesson again?" Usually, the answer is no.

I remember failing at not finishing a college degree. I was ambitious when I started my undergraduate degree as a dance major thinking that I would go on to also finish a master's degree and PhD. After running out of money, I dropped out and threw all my hours at an associate's business degree just to feel better. I didn't feel better. I just had $17,000 in debt now.

The sense of failure I was feeling was societal. It's good to get a college degree, right? It's a privilege to have access to higher education, right? Even better if we get more than one degree. Degrees make us feel smart.

Did I need a degree? No. Did I think I needed one? Yes. Did I want one? Yes. Ironically, I later received an honorary doctorate for my humanitarian work.

For me, this dance came from a combination of growing up in a blue-collar neighborhood in Chicago but then transferring to a suburban high school in an affluent community where high academics were worshiped. I found myself in a place where the median income was highest in the United States. So the public schools were far more advanced than what I was used to.

I struggled academically and felt "less-than" until I worked my way up the school ladder of success. My peers had learned multiple languages in grammar school while I was just learning how to diagram sentences. Most of these kids were destined for Ivy Leagues universities; I had not even thought about education beyond high school.

This school completely changed my perspective. Previously, I thought my options were quite limited. I might become a secretary or factory worker or mom or teacher. All these are fine vocations or roles. But suddenly my horizon grew wider. Now my thoughts were focused on where I might attend college and what I might major in. It was exciting but also very new.

I chose a school that my peers thought was silly because it was a state university instead of a school like Harvard or Yale. I chose a major that my peers and parents thought was unrealistic because what could a degree in dance do for me? As usual, I bucked the status quo. I loved my college classes. I loved that I got to go to college at all.

Dropping out of college a couple of times felt like a failure at the time.

Humans are continuously in a natural state of learning, growing, evolving and expanding. Failure is a big part of this. If everything went well all the time, we wouldn't grow much.

Coaching Tip:

Have fun with your failures. Look upon them lightly.

Qualitarian Question:

What's the last great lesson you learned from a failure?

18

Authenticity

Are you the same no matter who you're with, what you're doing and where you are? This, to me, is the essence of authenticity. In other words, you are the same no matter what.

Do you change who you are when you're at work or church or school or home? Are you a chameleon to conform to others? Do you hide who you really are in certain settings?

The content of your conversations might change. I'm not necessarily going to talk to my mom about my sex life the way I would to a friend, but being authentic is not changing how I am—no matter the company I'm keeping.

Qualitarians are true to their nature. Expressing our true selves is not always easy or safe. Coming out as gay is a good example of this. It might make you lose friends or the approval of family members. This can prevent us from speaking and behaving in ways that are genuine to ourselves.

The best parts of your personality shine when you're being yourself. But we don't always feel safe revealing who we really are. I don't mean that I'm going to have the same conversation with my mom that I would with my sister. But I try to be as authentically me no matter what. In other words, I might talk about my sex life with a friend but not a parent.

Trust me. This is not always easy. But honestly, it's even harder NOT to be yourself. It's stressful to hide and pretend. When I started telling people that I was bisexual, I lost some friends. I remember telling a friend at work that I was planning to have an open marriage, and she basically went around the office encouraging coworkers not to attend my wedding. I was shocked and hurt. Were these true friends? No, but it still hurt my feelings.

It stung because I remember trusting this person enough to share that I am bisexual which is why I was entering an open marriage. She talked about her uncle being gay and how she "still loved him no matter what." I felt safe enough to open up to her, and she twisted this information into a tool of dismissal, judgment and rejection.

Living an authentic life is sometimes expressed with what we wear and how we decorate our homes and even bumper stickers on our cars. As an animal advocate, I have worn "Fur is Dead" buttons on my winter coats standing next to fur-wearing colleagues in elevators at work. I've had my car vandalized for having stickers like "Meat is Dirty" on it.

I also highly respect Indigenous people who hunt for their own meat and wear animal hides and skins from their hunts. This is also an authentic part of me. Do I love animals? Yes. Do I sometimes eat animals? Yes. This is a contradiction but also there's an authenticity in my admittance of this.

I have various queer pride t-shirts that I feel more comfortable wearing in certain settings. Does this mean that I'm not being authentic when I'm not wearing them in some countries or with differing communities? Maybe. I am, at least, aware that I am choosing my clothing and language and behavior differently when I do.

There's a lot of freedom in completely being yourself. There's also a lot of risk. Sometimes it's not safe to share who we really are. I admire, so much, those who are unapologetically themselves. I have been so inspired by people who know exactly who they are and express exactly who they are.

Imagine you being that person for someone else.

Coaching Tip:

Ask yourself how much you're showing up in life truly as who you are.

Qualitarian Question:

What might happen if you start showing others exactly who you are?

19

Loss Aversion

We are all afraid of losing things. Losing people in our lives. Losing our youth. This can actually be motivating when we harness its power.

When people you know are celebrating something in their lives, are you wishing it was you celebrating? Do you find them boasting about their successes? Are you jealous or envious? This is very telling. It's natural to want what others have. But do you find the accomplishments of others bothersome to you?

The first time I ever played bingo in an official way, I won on my very first game. This was in one of those very serious bingo halls. Chain-smokers had at least 10 cards in front of them for each winning cycle. I had just turned 18, so I was old enough. I was overwhelmed at first with the size of the place and the very-loud speakers, yelling out numbers and letters.

I sat down with my sheets and ink push markers, and sure enough, had B-I-N-G-O on my first try. The regulars around me were not pleased with my beginner's luck. In fact, the thought of them losing to me was more intense than if they had won themselves. I felt their stares and glares as I went up to the front to collect my money. Later that night, even my boyfriend was jealous of my big wad of cash I brought to his house. Instead of being happy for me, he was almost confused about it. Sometimes a reward for someone else can feel like a loss for us.

Try this: Think of something that you can accomplish within the next thirty days. Now imagine how you might reward yourself if you actually accomplish it.

For example, maybe you'd like to be more disciplined in your exercise regimen or weekly food prep. Maybe you'd like to gain or lose a few pounds. Maybe you'd like to ask for a raise at work. Whatever it is, form this in your mind.

Now imagine the "prize" you will receive if you do it. Maybe it's $500. Maybe it's a trip. Maybe it's a spa day.

Now imagine someone you really dislike. At the end of the thirty days, you receive the prize if you accomplish your goal. But if you don't, the person you dislike does. Yikes!

The threat of losing something we want to someone else can be more motivating. Surprisingly, this can be more motivating than us receiving the reward.

Coaching Tip:

Break your goals down into manageable timeframes like days, weeks or months.

Qualitarian Question:

What prize would you like to receive in thirty days?

20

Make Up Your Mind More Easily

It's easy to make a decision when we ask ourselves straightforward questions. Think of something you really want. Like really, really want.

Maybe you want to get married. Maybe you want to become an entrepreneur. Maybe you want to travel more. When you have a decision to make, now you have a great measuring tool.

Does this **support or sabotage** this other thing I want? For example, if I want to do well on a test tomorrow morning, does staying up late to watch more TV sabotage my desire to test well by preventing me from feeling well-rested?

If I want to start dating, am I saying "Yes" to invitations to parties or my friends trying to set me up?

Does this **help or hinder** what I want? If you want to travel in a couple of months and need to save money to do so, does spending extra money on clothes make sense?

Making decisions can feel daunting, but this technique simplifies it quite nicely. While writing this book, I asked myself if it would be helpful to hire a book coach and join a writing group. Do these actions help me to stay on track? One of my tendencies is to turn in work quickly, like a blog post or online article. I've had to ask myself, "Would it be helpful for me to sleep on it and take another look at this written piece tomorrow instead of turning it in early today?"

When I'm walking my dogs at the park, I ask myself if it supports my health to walk longer instead of taking a shorter route. These little decisions throughout the day accumulate into bigger changes.

It's funny how I hate to walk uphill. I dread it. The parking lot at the park sits atop a huge former golf course. So I walk my dogs downhill first then uphill back to the car. Every single time, I have a disdain for the uphill parts. It's a mental game that I never win. I laugh at myself because I get so angry, especially when it's super hot and super uncomfortable as a result.

We all dread certain things that could easily be experienced in a more positive light. For example, I could put myself in a state of gratitude that I have a body that functions well and that I have two strong legs for walking. I'm reminded of this when I think about a very close friend of mine who can no longer walk. His paralysis is a result of gunshot wounds. I'm pretty sure he would love the chance to walk with his own legs instead of using a wheelchair.

The same goes for breathing. I love to take deep breaths of fresh air outdoors. It reminds me that some people have lung issues. I'm grateful for this body of mine. I appreciate the time I take to make sure my dogs are getting the activity they and I both need. *Qualitarians* consider this in their everyday lives.

Making a decision to take a longer walk or appreciating the walk you're on is compelling. Making other life decisions is similar. The bigger the decision, the more time it might take to make it. The more meaningful the decision, the more mindful you might be while making it.

I believe that adult humans like a choice of three. Children do well with a choice of two things. I have asked my children, "Do you want corn or peas with your dinner?" and they answered pretty easily with their preference. If I had asked them, "Do you want corn or peas or asparagus," it's more confusing. If I were to ask, "What vegetable do you want for dinner?"—that also might be even more confusing because it's too vast for a young child.

As an adult, I've noticed that I like having a choice of three things, maybe where I want to vacation or what I want to order on a menu or what I choose to wear. One option isn't really a choice! Two choices feel limiting because it's an "either-or." But three choices feels more manageable.

The next time you're trying to make a decision, try this: Give yourself three options. Maybe you're deciding who to hang out with or what to do while spending time with friends. Maybe you're choosing a new job. A new place to live. An adventure to try. Before making a decision, have three distinct options in mind. Then see if this "choice of three" technique works for you.

Coaching Tip:

When making a decision, relax your body and trust what comes.

Qualitarian Question:

What has been in the way of something you really want?

PART SIX:
FINANCIAL

21

Money Mindset

Have you ever won a prize and felt that surge of adrenalin? This is your bio-chemical response to a money surprise. Did you know that you can bring more money into your life by recreating this sensation? Since we attract what we are versus what we want, we simply need to "be" those things.

Do you worry about money? Do you wake up in the morning stressing about money and fall asleep at night worrying some more? This is just the worst feeling ever!

Instead, try thinking like someone wealthy. Feeling it. Acting like it. What would a wealthy person be thinking? Acting? Believing? Feeling? What does a wealthy person's day look like? If you had a million dollars extra in your bank account, what would you do? How would you feel? What would you think? This is the "acting as if" part. Yes, it's a form of imagination and pretending. But remember: your brain doesn't know the difference. It takes everything literally.

Here's a fun exercise I use with my coaching clients. I hand them an envelope and have them imagine $500 in it. I tell them they must spend this money on themselves within the next two days or it disappears. They can't pay bills with it and they can't give it away.

What would you do with your $500? Maybe you would go shopping. Perhaps you would treat yourself to a spa day. Maybe you go to a fancy restaurant.

The point of this exercise is to get into the feeling of unexpected, extra money. This playful moment in your mind will start manifesting more money!

Here's an indicator of how you're feeling about money. What are your thoughts when you're checking your checking account balance? How are you feeling when you swipe your card at the grocery store? When my husband and I go to Target or Costco, he looks away when the total shows because he doesn't want to know how much we've spent.

Maybe you're angry about how much groceries cost. Maybe you're frustrated about how you can't afford what you really want. Maybe you're disappointed about how life feels like a "chasing the dollar" rat race.

Instead, try feeling appreciation when you spend money. I have enough. I have more than enough. I am grateful that I can feed myself. This positive energy goes a long way when it comes to universal abundance.

I remember making a peanut butter and jelly sandwich for my daughter when she was young. I was crying tears of joy in my kitchen. I was able to afford food for us. I was safe. I wasn't hungry. At the time, I was a single mom and we didn't have much. But we had enough. Have you ever had that giddy feeling when unloading your groceries?

When I was little, my mom was a member of the National Consumer Panel which meant that she earned things like small kitchen appliances if she tracked her food purchases. What this meant was that before putting our groceries away, she would track the name, price, description, size, weight and reason for each and every item. I remember thinking that this was A LOT of work for very little reward.

It reminds me of Green Stamps that her mother used—and coupons in general. Trust me, I love a great coupon. No matter how much money I have, I thoroughly enjoy a discount on my gas and a great Walgreens coupon. Occasionally I imagine a day that I wouldn't care about coupons at all. We shall see.

So much of our money mindset comes from our childhood. What did our parents say about money? I remember my stepmom saying, "There's always something," when it comes to having to spend money. I grew up in a blue-collar neighborhood in Chicago where people lived paycheck-to-paycheck at best. People pinched pennies. People lived hand-to-mouth. It seemed to be a culture of scarcity that permeated our lives.

On the other hand, we had roofs over our heads and clothes to wear and didn't go hungry—the way some do. It felt like a "just enough" way of life.

What did you learn about money in your childhood household? Maybe that it doesn't grow on trees. Maybe that there's never enough to go around. Maybe that your money is already spent before it's earned!

I knew that my money mindset was changing when I went to an expo with a friend. I'm not normally much of a shopper, but maybe that's because I don't see myself that way. We walked past many booths of fun things to purchase. Just when we were about to leave I was very drawn to a booth.

I don't wear jewelry, but this booth of beautiful bracelets caught my eye. Each one was a different color made of Swarovski crystals and I immediately picked up the amber one and put it on my left wrist. There were no price tags. But instead of asking, "How much does this cost?"—what came out of my mouth surprised me. What I heard myself say was, "How much am I spending?"

In this moment, I realized how far I had come. I reached into my purse and handed over my debit card without taking the bracelet off. She responded, "$199."

The old me would have put the bracelet back and said, "Thanks." The new me just paid for it. And when I wear that bracelet now, it feels so good. I didn't hesitate. I didn't question. I didn't roll my eyes. I didn't have that "well maybe next time" feeling.

A couple of years later, I accidentally paid "too much" for a purse in a foreign airport. Normally, I head to TJ Maxx and spend $40 or so on my purses—that I hang on to and use exclusively for at least a year. I thought this airport purse was about $40 until I checked my bank balance and realized that I spent $189 on the purse. I freaked out a bit.

I couldn't even use the purse for a while because it upset me. I was highly aware that I had some money and worth issues to work through. After a couple of weeks, my son asked me why I wasn't using it yet. This prompted me to take it off my shelf and switch over my purse stuff to this new one. It felt good. I felt like I deserved it.

You might spend way more on purses or whatever, but notice how you feel when you purchase things. Are you feeling guilty? Are you feeling worthy? Are you feeling indulgent? Notice how you're feeling and what you're thinking. This is so telling about where we are regarding money.

"Money is simply spiritual energy in motion," is what Gay Hendricks says. He's one of my favorite relationship coaches who wrote the book, *The Big Leap*. I think of this quote often and challenge myself to consider that money is not paper and coin. It's tied into our sense of security and safety. It's energetic.

Some of us don't spend money on ourselves at all. When you shop, is your cart full of things for other people? I know I walk around stores thinking, "Oh, my daughter would love that," and, "I'm going to get that for my friend." It's not good or bad to do this. But it's worth considering whether you could be more generous with yourself.

Coaching Tip:

Notice how you feel the next time you pay a bill. Are you mad at the vendor?

Qualitarian Question:

What would more money do for you?

22

Financial Hangovers

How does your money matter to you? Are you continually stressed about money no matter how much you have? Are you content with your bank balance?

In my coaching practice, I notice that my clients wake up worrying about money and go to sleep stressing about money. They check their checking account first thing in the morning to make sure they didn't bounce a check. They tend to have what I call "financial hangovers" after returning from a vacation or shopping spree at Target.

These clients might overspend on a weekend or on a trip. They dread looking at their bank apps on Monday mornings. They cringe when they log in; their eyes wince as they hope for the best.

This kind of stress creates more strain than they realize. This stress is affecting their relationships and their health, both physically and mentally. One of the most common topics that coaching clients bring to their session relates to money.

Because money is never about money, it's important to keep in mind that money sometimes represents power or control—sometimes lack or insecurity. For example, if you grew up not having much, you might bring that into your adulthood—the sense of not having enough.

It's little things, like the quality of your salt and pepper shakers. Not everyone is a cook or foodie, but you can tell a lot about a person based on whether they have cheapo shakers or slightly nicer ones that freshly grind peppercorns. Do you have more than one kind of salt? Kosher or flake salt for certain recipes and table salt for everything else?

My son and I bought my husband a nice peppermill as a gift. You know, from one of those fancy kitchen appliance stores. What a difference it makes when you don't have to bite down on a big piece of pepper or use the overly ground kind. Eggs in the morning have a whole new meaning.

Speaking of breakfast eggs, are you purchasing the least expensive ones at the store or maybe the pasture-raised ones that are just a couple of dollars more? Maybe you're driving to a farmers market to get the really good ones. Perhaps you'll decide to have farm-fresh eggs with chickens of your own.

These seemingly small money matters make a difference. Because I currently live in a more rural area, I have become very spoiled eating fresh eggs from local farmers. I don't think I can ever go back to store-bought! Being a *Qualitarian* is about eating the most delicious eggs and seasoning them with high-quality salt and pepper. It's so simple in most ways.

If you're a smoothie drinker, it would be about the quality of ingredients in your blend. If you're a bagel lover, are you using your favorite cream cheese and toppings?

I remember being so broke in my 20s, working for a prestigious nonprofit in downtown Chicago. I couldn't afford an expensive lunch each day. I adored the days when I splurged to buy a cup of potato leek soup from the deli downstairs in the gorgeous Monadnock building, famous for not having burned down during the Great Chicago Fire of 1871. It had 16 stories with marble floors and gold-plated mailshoots.

The toasted sesame bagels with green-olive cream cheese downstairs were divine. The croissants across the street were light and fluffy. I savored every bite when I treated myself to these. Most of the renters in this building are law firms and nonprofits, so many of the customers at these eateries can easily afford their meals. But for me, it was something really special.

When I later worked in Oak Park, Illinois, famous for Frank Lloyd Wright homes, I had two favorite spots to eat. Although I was making more money at this job, I was still the only working parent in my home so my budget was tight. Did I bring peanut butter and jelly sandwiches to work most days? Yes. Did I want to? No.

There was this great French bakery owned by a Vietnamese family that served "Tofu Stir Fry" for lunch-but only on Tuesdays. This became my favorite day of the week because this dish was so incredible (and luckily) also affordable. The name of this dish might not excite you, but trust me—it was delectable.

I was a vegetarian at the time working for *Vegetarian Times* magazine, so of course, I had to do my research. It was more like a soup with comforting rice noodles and julienned carrots and cabbage. The broth was perfect. The tofu was long strips of crispy yet pillowy pieces. I nearly had to keep my eyes closed the whole time eating this dish.

What added to the experience was dining at the bakery versus getting takeout. Getting to know this family. Smelling all the smells. Appreciating all the nuances of the meal. It was such a pleasurable experience for me.

My coworkers and I also loved a local Italian place called Trattoria Peppino in neighboring Elmwood Park, Illinois. Once a week, we would order up some delicious pasta and get it delivered. My favorite dish of theirs is Baby Shell Besciamella with a homemade red cream sauce. This was decades ago and I still remember this meal.

It's still in business so, you're welcome. Because I didn't make much money at my editorial assistant job, this was an effortful expense for me and totally worth every bite. In fact, most of my coworkers didn't make a lot, because publishing doesn't pay very well. We all enjoyed our pastas with huge smiles on our faces without a lot of talking during these lunches.

Money is relative. When we have only $50 to spend on groceries, we cut corners. When we have only $5 for lunch, we might have to split an entrée with a friend. When I was a kid, I didn't get much allowance but I usually would buy myself a 50-cent gravy bread from my absolute favorite place to eat on Chicago's Northwest side, Roma's. It's basically French bread dunked into au jus from the Italian Beef sandwich meat containers. Pure heaven.

Coaching Tip:
Consider what you really want to eat when purchasing meals and dining out.

Qualitarian Question:
How do you spend your food dollars?

23

What's Your Worth?

A huge part of becoming a *Qualitarian* is fully understanding your worth, financially and otherwise.

Claiming it.

Owning it.

Requesting it.

Have you noticed that your relationships have improved as you've aged? If so, this might be a result of you improving. Think back to a previous lover or friend or spouse. The person you were back then was a good match for that person back then, but both of you are now different people. The more you grow and expand, the juicier your relationships become. This can also hold true for your financial situation.

When I made the switch from working at a nonprofit to working for *Vegetarian Times* magazine, it was more of a necessity than anything else. My husband at the time was home with our daughter, so it was important for me to bring home as much vegetarian bacon as possible, haha.

Sometimes when we're young, we will accept low salary offers because we are so eager to get hired. Especially if it's an employer we really want to work for, we get giddy when offered a job.

When my daughter was 10 months old, I started back with some dance classes and decided to volunteer at an animal advocacy organization since it was just a block or two away. After a couple of weeks of stuffing envelopes and other administrative tasks, an employee asked me if I was looking for work. I responded with a maybe, and she basically offered me a job on the spot as a programming associate.

I was so excited that this nonprofit was going to pay me for time I was offering for free that I forgot to ask what the salary was. I called her when I got home and she responded with, "Oh, sorry. It's $11 per hour."

Needless to say, I was disappointed by this number but still wanted to work there. After a year or so, I headed into my executive director's office to ask for more money. Granted, she made 10 times what I was making. I knew this because salaries of registered nonprofits are public record.

I let her know that I need a certain amount to justify being a single-income household. I gave her all the reasons why—including that I was a devoted employee and increased their fundraising efforts.

She turned me down, citing all kinds of blah-blah-blah reasons. I remember this feeling so vividly, being denied something so reasonable and so deserving. It fueled me. I immediately headed to the conference room to make a couple of phone calls.

The first call was to a respected colleague who served on their board of directors. I explained the situation and he agreed with me that it was time to go. He had recommendations for me and said he could make a couple of calls, but I let him know that I had some ideas of my own.

I sat there for a few minutes thinking about where I really wanted to work. Being a vegetarian at the time, *Vegetarian Times* magazine came to mind. Also, I love magazines. I like reading, writing, editing and proofreading. I enjoy preparing meals and dining out. This would be a great fit for me.

I called their office and asked the receptionist if there were any job openings. This is a good technique, by the way. Don't ask for Human Resources. Sometimes the receptionist knows the inside scoop.

She told me that they hadn't yet posted these positions but there were three soon-to-be openings for an editorial assistant, inventory manager and sales manager assistant. I realized, in that moment, that I could probably do all three of those jobs in one. I sent off my resumé and landed an interview with the magazine's founder, Paul Obis.

I was nervous because I really wanted it. Paul was a sweet and eccentric guy, so I enjoyed his company as he asked me all kinds of questions about why I was interested in working for him. I mentioned reasons, like deeply caring for animals and being a wordsmith.

He was barefoot during the interview which I thought was cool, and he smiled a lot then offered me a job on the spot. He initially said that he could pay me $19 per hour but then adjusted that to $22 hourly because he knew that my current nonprofit job offered great benefits. So I basically walked out of his office doubling my salary.

This was a big lesson for me because I could have easily stayed at a lower-paying job because I enjoyed it and liked my coworkers. I was told "No." So I actively pursued something better for myself.

After several weeks at my new position, I attended a holiday party at a coworker's home. It was attended mostly by editors and their partners. I highly respected these people and remember diminishing my role when someone asked me, "So what do you do at the magazine?" I replied, "Oh, I'm just an editorial assistant." My peers immediately corrected me by saying things like, "What do you mean? We couldn't do our jobs without you," or, "Why are you describing it like that?"

Yes, another lesson in understanding my worth. I felt proud on the inside yet expressed it as less desirable on the outside. This is such an interesting disconnect. It taught me to claim my worth and understand my value.

I recently doubled my coaching rates by offering 30-minute sessions instead of hourlong ones. Not one of my clients balked. After coaching professionally for 17 years now, I have become very efficient in the first 30 minutes with my clients. It's like the three-bite rule. The first three bites of a meal, especially a dessert, are the best. So why keep going?

Coaching Tip:

Volunteering and interning at an organization is a great way "in" sometimes leading to a paid position.

Qualitarian Question:

Are you getting paid what you're worth?

PART SEVEN:
ENVIRONMENTAL

24

Natural Cycles

Are you following the natural cycles of the world? Are you spending time outdoors to notice the natural rhythms of the day and night? When was the last time you watched a sunrise or looked at the moon at length?

In Honduras in Central America, there is a beautiful expression, "Give it to the sea and the sand." What this means is that the earth will take your pain for you. I went on a spiritual retreat there in 2013. During our time there, a Guatemalan shaman facilitated a beautiful fire ceremony for us. She explained how the valley before us can receive what we no longer desire to have in our lives.

She, Aumrak, had us bring something physical that represented someone or something we wanted to release. At the time, I had a nasty client who was very demanding and negative. This client had gifted me with a piece of jewelry I didn't want (and didn't like). So that's what I brought.

We stood at the edge of a vast valley in the mountains, deep in the rainforest. One at a time, we threw our items into the dark night. Mine was that bracelet and it felt like it went hundreds of yards in front of me. I felt a sudden lifting of my soul and a huge sense of relief. It was powerful for me because I tend to hold onto things too long.

As a professional coach, I encourage my clients to lay "belly down" outside if they're feeling vulnerable. I encourage them to cry their eyes out if needed. Being face down allows the land to absorb their challenging emotions. Face up is more of a receiving mode. Lying face down is a giving mode. Give it to the land. She will gladly take it for you.

Are you a sunrise or sunset person? Are you getting enough fresh air, sunshine and moonlight in your everyday existence? What about "the outdoors" is most enjoyable for you?

As a child, I remember being outdoors and feeling a sense of relief. In many ways nature saved me. I had a tough upbringing but was fortunate enough to spend a whole lot of my childhood outdoors.

We went hiking, camping, backpacking, rock climbing, snow skiing—you name it! One of my favorite things about hiking was sitting on a large log above a rolling stream in Colorado and watching it go by. This was so incredibly comforting and relaxing to me.

I am a forest person. I am lucky enough to have a great park nearby where I walk my dogs in a mini forest of sorts. The trees are so beautiful and the wind speaks to me. I swear I saw a fairy once come out around a tree!

What kind of outdoors do you enjoy? Are you a mountain person? A desert person? A beach person? A forest person like me? If you enjoy water, do you prefer saltwater or freshwater? Oceans, lakes or rivers?

On a trip to Panama in Central America once, I sat on the beach at midnight under a full moon with two great friends. It was one of the best nights of my life. We laughed and talked and soaked up the moonlight like it was water after a long thirst. We sat on lawn chairs and had to dodge hermit crabs heading back to our huts to sleep. I didn't want the night to end.

The soft waves lapping at our feet were so grounded and comforting. The sand was soft yet so stable below us. I heard a great analogy from a quantum physicist once about the present moment. He described himself standing on a beach shore and how the sand is the past. The water is the future and the moving, foamy line of water going back and forth represents the present moment. It's fleeting and you can't grab it. Nature easily puts us in this state of being.

Spending time in nature is a cure for our soul. It can provide mental clarity, emotional uplifting and overall grounding. When was the last time you spent time in nature truly appreciating it?

Being a *Qualitarian* is about enjoying the qualities of nature. Enjoy the fresh air. Enjoy the sunshine. Enjoy the moonlight. Enjoy the sunsets. Enjoy the rain. Enjoy the heat. Enjoy the snow. Enjoy the sounds. Enjoy it all.

Coaching Tip:

Try spending at least eight minutes outdoors every day.

Qualitarian Question:

What messages do you receive from nature?

25

Indoor Spaces

We spend more time indoors than out. Is your indoor environment cluttered? Does it bring you delight? Our time indoors dictates so much of our moods and energy shifts.

What's your favorite part of your indoor space? What part of your home feels best to you? Do you have a safe comfy spot all to yourself?

Think about your dream home. Does it have a fireplace? Maybe a fountain? Maybe a large soaking tub? A hammock? Maybe a huge cook's kitchen? Or maybe a great reading nook?

As a young child, I remember reading this picture book about a house and a family. All the furniture was highly functional and everything had its place. There was a phonebook on a shelf below the phone table. There was a well-placed rug wherever one was needed. In hindsight, this house had a very minimalistic look that I enjoy in my current home. This book imprinted quite a lot on me. I recall feeling a sense of calm looking at this environment.

Most of us are caught in a cycle of clutter and chaos. We have too much. We own too much. We shop too much. We head to Target, not really needing anything in particular and wind up coming home with hundreds of dollars of stuff that slightly alters our space and therefore slightly delights us—for a brief time.

I heard somewhere that the urge to keep changing our indoor spaces like moving furniture or rearranging artwork is a trauma response. I've also heard that it can reflow stagnant energy. We're all different. So this differs for everyone. *Qualitarians* are focused on the quality of their environments.

Oprah is known for saying that one of her initial big purchases after making it big was "thick thirsty towels" because she always had thin old towels growing up. The first time I ever had a big chunk of money was just after my freshman year at college, when my dad sold my stock I owned worth $1800. That was A LOT of money to me back then.

I was just about to move to California from Iowa to attend UCLA, and I went shopping at a small-town department store called Younkers. I went straight to the home department and felt all the plush thirsty towels, even though it would have been much smarter for me to buy them in California. I bought, not the most expensive but one of the more expensive bath towels in a few different colors. This made me feel so grown up. Sharing bath towels with siblings is no fun growing up.

Now, one of my favorite indoor activities is using a fresh clean towel after a shower. I even have a way I dry myself off and cover my hair and tuck in the towel a certain way on my head. It's divine.

Another *Qualitarian* trait of mine is changing my bed sheets often, like three times a week. Some people find this excessive, but I absolutely love the feel of clean sheets and clean blankets and clean pillow cases. Yes, I like quality fabrics but I don't go crazy with thread counts and designer brands. I just make sure that I enjoy the color and the feel.

I'm a firm believer that each person in a home should have a sacred space of their own—somewhere to go to be alone if needed. A place for your own things. A room of your own, as Virginia Woolfe would say. For me, this is my office. I have my favorite artwork, my collection of animal figurines, including Zuni fetishes carved by Native Americans of the American Southwest. I have a beautiful view from my window, overlooking my acre yard with a stream and a forest full of birds and animals. It's my favorite indoor space at home. Do you have a favorite space of your own?

Our indoor space dictates our moods. Are your favorite colors around you? Is your couch comfortable? Do you have a great bed to sleep in? Do you enjoy the artwork at home?

A *Qualitarian* is someone who enjoys spending time indoors in a comfortable environment.

Coaching Tip:

Do an audit on your home. What can go? What might be missing?

Qualitarian Question:

What's your favorite thing about your home?

26

Trading Places

In my professional coach training sessions, I do a guided meditation exercise with my students where they "trade places" with someone else for a week. First, I get them in a relaxed state. Next, before explaining anything, I ask them to pick someone they know, someone alive. Then I describe that they are going to live this person's life for an entire week.

They will eat their meals, sleep in their beds, get around in their forms of transportation, spend time with their people, wear their clothes, think their thoughts, feel their feelings, etc. They will work at their jobs, have their dreams, embody their bodies, experience their mindsets, go about their days in their ways, etc.

This is an exercise in empathy. It's a visceral meditation in which my students learn to walk in someone else's shoes for a week. How much is in their bank account if they have one? What are their thoughts about that amount? What is it like to prepare and taste their foods? How does it feel to feel their feelings? What sensations do they notice most?

They might notice how anxious someone is or how calm they are. They might reflect on what it's like to be part of a different size family or completely unique marriage. They might realize that they are living someone's wonderful existence or someone's nightmare. Maybe they sense a different level of stress or stressors about different aspects of life.

After a solid 20 minutes or so into this exercise, we "trade places" again—not back to normal—but this other person now steps into your life. This is quite the turnaround. The environment flips.

Now this other person is driving your car if you have one, taking the bus or getting your ride. Sometimes my students quickly realize how dirty their car is or how messy their apartment is. (No, they don't get a chance to clean up or change anything before the switch.)

They might feel bad that the bed sheets are dirty or that the fridge is only stocked with boring foods. They might be delighted that this person gets to kiss their spouse or hug their kids. They might worry about this other person having to feel their body shame or face their demons. They might wonder what it's like to think about their inspiring thoughts or have their funny sense of humor. They might relish the thought of this person enjoying their backyard or vacation.

My students typically notice that they would prefer to have their recipients experience something different. They would prefer them to enjoy their job or be a better friend. They would prefer them to savor a cup of tea versus rushing through it. They would prefer them to take a long soak in their tub instead of quickly showering. They would prefer them to love their lives.

This is a great exercise for realizing how we would wish for others what we don't do for ourselves. This reminds me of when my mom spent a lot of money replacing the carpet in my childhood home before putting it on the market to sell. She was disappointed when she realized that she didn't do that for herself while she lived there.

What are you not doing for yourself that you would wish for someone else?

Coaching Tip:

Since your environment is a reflection of you, take some time soon to rearrange some furniture or declutter a space.

Qualitarian Question:

How would you feel if someone stepped into your life today?

27

The Dog Collector

Our environments are more than our indoor and outdoor spaces. They include the 'who' as well. The people, the pets, the plants. These are all a significant part of our environments.

Qualitarians are purposeful about the company they keep, whether it be friends, family, acquaintances, coworkers, animals and more. Who we spend our time with is as vital as how we spend our time with them.

During my coaching sessions, I sometimes notice this 'not wanting to go home' tendency in my clients. They dread going home to their people. Gauging their stress about going home is a barometer of their relationships.

I once had a client who called herself "'The Sandwich Generation." For her it meant that she lived and cared for her young children and elderly parents. She called herself "the bologna in the middle."

She described dreading going home after work because the kids would immediately pounce on her as soon as she walked through the front door, clamoring for her attention. Then her parents would need things from her. All she wanted was to relax when she got home from a long day's work.

She repeatedly asked for relief by asking, "Can I please just have 10 minutes to get undressed, check the mail and go to the bathroom?" Her family didn't oblige. Even her husband did not seem helpful because he was so ready to hand things off to her.

Our homes are our sacred places. My coaching clients remind me of my own similar situations. I remember when my daughter was very young, and I would walk into the house after a long commute and a long day. All I wanted was to unwind and have a moment to myself before jumping into daily chores or cooking dinner.

We used cloth diapers, and I distinctly remember being sick of the smell of urine that seemed to follow me home after taking the subway (that also smelled like urine). It's like I couldn't get away from the smell.

I have a theory called the "Friday Night Effect." It's simply the measure of whether someone wants to go home on a Friday night. The end of the week is even more of a litmus test for the comfort or discomfort someone feels about heading back to their home after a week's work.

I have a client who instantly turns on the TV when she comes home each night because she lives alone and finds this comforting. She kicks off her shoes upon entering her front door and puts on CNN. The show stays on until she goes to bed. She describes it like it's a companion for her.

She doesn't like going home on Friday nights. For her, it's a reminder that she's still single. It's a reminder that she's still grieving her last boyfriend. Their breakup was tough on her and she misses having someone to spend time with on a Friday night.

It's these small yet subtle events that let us know where we are regarding something. This client is filling her apartment with noise to prevent having to hear the silence of it just being her in her space.

When I coach a single client, I ask if they have "someone to love" because humans have three basic needs—this being one of them. This "someone" can be a plant or a person or even a pet. Someone to care about and care for. I might even recommend a weekly massage for my single clients because humans also need to be touched to thrive.

This particular client didn't have a pet or any plants, so she decided to get both. She started with a kitten that eventually turned into two cats. She bought some flowering plants for her balcony, and these small steps really made a difference for her. She now has something to come home to.

The other two basic human needs have to do with needing "something to do" and having "something to look forward to." I have clients who have one of two of these needs, but not all.

A retired client of mine used to be super busy with work tasks but now feels bored with days full of zero tasks. He used to look forward to retirement, but now feels a sense of emptiness. I asked him what he might like to "do" with his newfound extra time, and he finally realized that he wanted to do some volunteering. He chose to rock babies at the hospital! Yes, there are programs for this.

Another one of my retired clients started walking dogs at the local animal shelter. Another one started going to the library to read to kids. Both of these activities are doubly helpful because the dog walker was getting exercise and the library reader was keeping her mind sharp.

Having "something to look forward to" is also vital for a *Qualitarian*. Maybe it's a birthday celebration coming up or lunch with a friend. Perhaps it's a vacation or finishing a great book. Without this anticipation, we stagnate.

My "Friday Night Effect" theory came from my own experience. During my first marriage, I remember not wanting to go home one Friday night. My daughter was seven at the time, so I usually looked forward to coming home to her, but my relationship with her dad was not as healthy.

We didn't always have an unhealthy relationship, but we were going through a rough patch. I left work on that Friday and headed to see a movie by myself. I was so looking forward to the movie adaptation of Anne Rice's book, *Interview with a Vampire,* with Brad Pitt and Tom Cruise.

Even after the movie, I still didn't want to go home so I drove over to my friend's house in the other direction. This was pre-cellphone, and when I walked into my friend's house they said that my husband was trying to get a hold of me.

I called home from their landline and he told me that my friend, Kent, was eagerly trying to call me. I tried calling him but for hours there was no answer. I hung out with my friends and eventually headed home. My emotion at the time wasn't one of dread. It was more like indifference.

The next morning, I finally reached Kent who said that he had something really important he wanted to tell me the night before but now he wanted to wait to tell me. He had been drinking the night before and felt bold enough to say it, but now he didn't.

"Please," I begged him. He said, "I promise I'll tell you soon."

Well, soon never came because of his sudden, tragic passing just a few weeks later. One of the thoughts that flashed through my mind when I heard of his death was that I'll never get to learn what he wanted to tell me that night. It's been over 20 years now. And I still wonder.

It was at this moment that I realized that I didn't enjoy coming home to my husband. I felt displaced anger at him, thinking that, if he were a better husband, I would have come home that night and gotten the phone call. I deserved to hear what Kent wanted to say.

I know this is irrational. But, at the time, it was how I felt. This realization helped me to understand that my marriage was coming to an end. Our environments are made up of people we enjoy—and some we don't.

I have been known to collect a dog or two. I currently have three big dogs and love them big. There was a time when my ex-boyfriend and I bred wolfdogs. Crazy to some, but not to us.

My ex came home one day to three new dogs because I went through the newspaper classified ads worrying about dogs being given away for free. I drove around Los Angeles picking them up from unwanted homes.

My justification was that I was rehoming them, but in hindsight, I was more likely filling my environment with the unconditional love that dogs so often offer. I also gained a lot from caring for them.

With my clients, I ask about their pets and their people. I ask about their coworkers and social activities. We might have a lot of people around us, but are we enjoying those people? We might have a lot of friends, but are they high-quality relationships?

It's the same with tasks. We might have a lot to do, but it is really something we want to do. Maybe we're feeling obligated to do it—going through the motions. Life is too short for this.

Coaching Tip:

Fill your environments with people who add to your life.

Qualitarian Question:

Who are you choosing to spend time with?

PART EIGHT:
SPIRITUAL

28

Cosmic Yanks

Have you ever felt like the rug got pulled out from under you? I mean deeply. This is, by far, what I find most difficult in life. It feels like I'm being spiritually tested.

My best friend died suddenly. My boyfriend broke up with me and it felt as if I were dealing with a death. My dog got hit by a car and it was totally my fault. All kinds of hard things. I believe that we sign up for experiences and that we are living out a spiritual destiny.

What hard things have you experienced? What cosmic yanks have you endured?

A cosmic yank to me is a sudden occurrence of something that changes everything. It forces you to reconsider your life. It makes you realize how mortal you are.

Life is about loss. We get cosmically yanked throughout life. These yanks and losses feel like they come from some vast place, somewhere beyond us and our understanding. My best friend's death was such a teacher to me—but at an alarming cost.

Kent had just turned 30 years old and had a baby on the way. He was a geologist who traveled, doing gigs like mussel diving and river research. Kent was trying to make as much money as he could before his baby was born. So he headed to Washington State to earn some quick cash. The circumstances of his death are still a mystery, but basically there was foul play.

Kent was found alone on a boat. Most likely he had been drugged after being robbed of the few thousand dollars cash he'd been paid for a geology project. The thought of him dying alone still haunts me. The person I loved most in this world was gone. This was a spiritually defining moment for me.

I had never met someone like Kent, full of so much joy and humor. He was instantly my best friend the day we met on our first day of college at University of Iowa. He was from Dubuque, Iowa, and so fantastically handsome. Kent was a tall guy of Swedish descent and such a kind, compassionate person.

Meeting him was a spiritual experience. Having long talks with him were spiritual experiences. We used to sit for hours touching the tops of our foreheads together sharing our thoughts, feelings and insights. We used to play this fun game. One of us would lie down with our eyes closed trying to sense where the other one was hovering their hand. For hours, we would do this and laugh and talk and smile until our faces hurt.

My best friend's death is the hardest thing that's ever happened to me. When it happened, I remember thinking that the only thing worse would be if I lost my child. What pops in our heads at moments like these is very telling. The pain I felt in my body and in my soul was so excruciating! It was a sudden, unexpected death. And there's something unique about someone's passing when you don't get a chance to say goodbye.

The tragedy of his death, especially because he never got to meet his son in person, was devastating beyond belief. I would never wish this kind of experience on my worst enemy. I have not been the same since. Frankly, I've been pretty done with this world since. This cosmic yank has been a great teacher for me. It has taught me appreciation for the precious time we have with others. It has taught me to savor moments with people.

Kent was a spiritual man but not a religious man. He continues to speak to me. And I'm so grateful for this communication—even though it's fleeting. I get little glimpses of him now and then. His son, Caleb, is now in his 20s and, of course, looks just like him—tall and blonde and beautiful.

Experiences like these remind us that we are spiritual beings. We don't HAVE a spirit. We ARE a spirit. We don't HAVE a soul. We ARE a soul. This means that we are living spiritually and soulfully.

Have you had spiritual cosmic yanks that have forever changed you? If so, do you see them as spiritual lessons or something else entirely?

Coaching Tip:

Look at your life as a series of spiritual experiences.

Qualitarian Question:

What beauty lies within your pain?

29

Honor Your Ancestry

Do you feel connected to your ancestors? Do you know who they are?

Imagine that you are no longer here. Instead, you are crossed over into another plane of consciousness. Would you enjoy supporting your loved ones still alive?

I have a namesake. I was named after my aunt Desiré. But I never met her because she passed away when she was 13 years old. She was riding a bike and got hit by a truck. Her death certificate states that it was a "hit and run." But it's possible that the truck driver didn't even know he hit her.

I only have a few photos of her but I love looking at them. One photo is the screen saver image on my phone. I don't know a whole lot about her other than she was a dancer and that my father adored her. He was only eight when she died.

I think of her as my guardian angel. I love being named after her. I too, became a dancer, and I'm pretty sure I inherited some of her talent. I think about her being born in Chicago to fairly poor parents. I think about her mom who was born on a farm in Iowa. As a result of doing genealogy work, I think about her aunt Genevieve and her grandmother, Rosabella, who came down from Quebec, as a poor farmer.

The Iowa connection is interesting because I didn't know that this side of my family lived in Iowa when I chose the University of Iowa as my college. I remember calling both my parents on my first night in my dorm telling them about new friends I'd met. I told my dad that I met Jason from Knoxville, Iowa, and that he said his town was famous for its soapbox derbies. My dad said, "Oh, that's where my mom was born—just outside Des Moines."

Then when telling my mom about my new Iowan friends, she said, "My father was born in Sabula, Iowa—a river city near the Mississippi." I was stunned. How could I have not known this? Both sides of my family had connections to Iowa. No wonder I grew up obsessed with cows and corn! It's that familial ancestral memory we hold in our cells.

I also think about my grandfather who emigrated from Holland in the early 1900s. I think about his parents and their parents. What were they like? What were their dreams?

My father's mother, Marguerite, died of breast cancer when he was only three years old. My father's father, Willem, died from a stroke when my father was 11. I never met my grandparents on that side of my family, but I honor them just the same. I remember visiting her grave for the first time after extensive research to find it. My father went into foster care after a short stint at an orphanage. He only had a small box of momentos, including my grandfather's passport and naturalization papers along with just a few photos of his sister, mother and father.

Actually, there was only one photo of his mother. It was painful for my dad to talk about his family because of the heartbreak of his loss. Before Google, I did genealogy research and discovered where they are all buried. I first visited my Marguerite's grave in a very old Greek Orthodox cemetery just outside of Chicago, Illinois. One of the mysteries about her was why she converted to Catholicism on her deathbed.

Because she was "Catholic," and poor, she was buried in the back corner of this cemetery without a burial vault—just a coffin in the lumpy ground alongside the railroad tracks. I nervously followed the instructions from the office staff about where to drive and walk and step—a few yards this way and that. Just when I got to her spot, a beautiful black snake came out of the area where her coffin lay just feet below. I love snakes and I was sure this was a sign from her.

Years later, I traced the steps of my namesake, Desirée, in a Catholic cemetery that just so happens to be right across the street from where my grandmother is laid to rest. In fact, the same distance from the railroad tracks exactly. Marguerite's dying wish was that her children be baptized Catholic, so my aunt was buried in a Roman Catholic cemetery—but again, where the poor people were buried in the back corner.

Desirée is buried below people meaning that she was buried, then dirt was layered above her, then more people were buried, then dirt was layered above them. As a result, my dad couldn't do what he wished, which was to have head-stones made for both his sister and his mother.

Because I am named after Desirée, I thought I would feel something profound there. But actually, it was at my grandmother's grave that I felt something so deep. I felt connected to her in a very spiritual way.

I was surprised to see my grandfather's handwriting in both cemetery logs. There's something special and hyper-connecting to see a family member's inked signature on an old ledger. Having never met any three of these people, it instantly brought my mind into focus about how they were real people and not just names and dates on documents.

I love the thought that they are loving me and supporting me from the other side. Wouldn't you be doing the same for your family members? A *Qualitarian* honors ancestral lines.

Coaching Tip:

See your life as a continuation of family members who came before you.

Qualitarian Question:

Are you asking your ancestors for guidance?

30

Are You Really Ready?

A *Qualitarian* has to be capable, ready, able and willing to do something in order for it to actually happen. We need all four components for success. This is why so many folks do not follow through with New Year's Resolutions or goals they set for themselves. Pick a goal right now. Something you'd like to obtain or experience.

Are you **capable** of doing this? Are you mentally capable? Are you physically capable? For example, if you want to train for a marathon, do you have the mental capacity to do so when you hit your wall? If you want to drive a truck and deliver packages, are you capable of lifting heavy boxes up to 75 pounds?

Are you **ready** to do this? Let's say you want to start dating. Are you ready to open your heart? Are you ready to express your feelings? Are you ready to feel all the feels?

Are you **able** to do this? For example, are you able to get to work if you get a new job? Are you going to drive yourself, get a ride or take public transportation? Are you able to fill out an online application to find work?

Are you **willing** to do this? Are you willing to do what it takes to make something happen for yourself? Are you willing to learn about yourself? Are you willing to make compromises if needed?

I call this the CRAW Method—capacity, readiness, ability and willingness. If you don't have all four of these components in place, your goals will not be achieved. Most of us have some of these but not all four in place.

I had a coaching client once whose husband resisted going back to work after staying home with their children while they were young. Their agreement was that he would go back to work when their youngest child started kindergarten. He was capable, somewhat ready, able but not willing.

Because of his unwillingness, my client applied for jobs for him online. She even took an online certification pretending to be him so that she could add this to his resume—a resume that she wrote for him. His work history was impressive, so he got immediate responses to the posting online. He got hired over the phone. On his first day of training, she was so hopeful because this job was high-paying with great benefits.

He came home after his first training day saying he wouldn't go back because he didn't like some of his peers. This was an excuse. The truth is that he wanted to remain at home and not work. He was not willing to start a new job. This led to her giving an ultimatum: "You need to go back tomorrow and continue your training or you need to move out." Guess what he did? Yep. He moved out!

Is she happier now? Yes. Was she shocked? Yes. Did his actions let her know where his priority is? Yes.

Where might you be lacking in one of these areas? Maybe you want to get married. Maybe you're capable, able and willing—but not ready.

As a holistic coach, most of my clients get stuck with the willingness. They are capable but not willing. Able but not willing. Ready but not willing.

During a group coaching session for LGBT teenagers, I asked one of the participants about his readiness. He was describing someone he wanted to meet romantically. He was so excited. He was telling us about how this person would be handsome, kind and funny. He was smiling and laughing about it. Then I asked him to imagine this person walking in the door right now. His reaction was very telling: "I'm not ready!" It's totally okay that he wasn't ready. Already feeling able, capable and willing is part of getting there. If you do not have all four of these—capacity, readiness, ability and willingness—your goals will not be met.

Coaching Tip:
Ask yourself which of these four areas is missing from a current goal of yours.

Qualitarian Question:
What are you really ready for?

31

Naps Are Spiritual

During my second year at University of Iowa, I lived off campus in a cute Victorian home on a corner. It was just a block away from the famous cartoonist, Berke Breathed, who wrote the *Bloom County* comic strip. This somehow made my house cooler.

At first I lived upstairs with a roommate who later invited his girlfriend from Ireland to move in. So I moved onto the first floor where the rooms felt roomy with super high ceilings. My bedroom was a former parlor and was hexagonal shaped. I only had a twin bed up against a large window so the room felt extra spacious.

Upstairs, I noticed how my new Irish friend, Karin, set up her own bedroom, even though her boyfriend had his own. I enjoyed meeting this exotic creature from another land and was impressed when she asked me where the nearest walkable grocer was so she could buy fresh ingredients to make a veggie soup.

Karin explained that she needed her own space, or what Virginia Woolfe described as "a room of one's own." She was playing her own records in her own room with her own bed. I thought this was fantastic. So liberating.

In my new space downstairs, my kitchen had a cute formica table that my mom gave me with matching chairs. My fridge was stocked with my college essentials—like imitation crabmeat dip, lemonade, Doritos and strawberry Häagen Dazs ice cream. Cigarettes were on the counter: Benson & Hedges 100s.

Karin would sometimes come downstairs and sunbathe in the backyard on a quilted blanket. I had a little boombox playing cassette tapes and my favorite was *Blue Moves* by Elton John. This double album is fantastic though (unfortunately) not all the tracks made it to the CD version.

I lay down on my bed one afternoon just to close my eyes "for a second." The next thing I know, I'm in and out of sleep feeling the most luscious breeze on my face through my bedroom window and drifting off into La La Land. It was the kind of nap that felt spiritual. As I danced between beta, alpha and theta brain waves, I soaked up every morsel of this deep yet light rest. It was exquisite.

A *Qualitarian* knows naps can be spiritual. So can daydreams. Humans have this unique ability to just "be" when we choose it. Most of us are not choosing it at all. We're "doing" instead of "being."

When I first started writing *The Qualitarian*, my book coach did a guided visualization with me and a group of aspiring writers. In a relaxed state, I could see someone on an airplane reading this book! It was nighttime and the light above the passenger was lit, and they were smiling and pondering while reading it. This image has motivated me to finish this book.

My book coach's name is Tisha Morris, who is also a literary agent and entertainment attorney. She is an incredible source of inspiration to me. One of the many things I've learned from her is the difference between authors and writers. By Tisha's definition, an author basically writes to be read whereas a writer must write no matter what. She is this kind of writer where she would pick up a napkin at a coffee shop to continue writing if she ran out of paper.

I think that I'm an author because I want my words to reach others. I don't write for writing's sake. I don't journal. I only journal if it's a part of a workshop or something that's assigned. It's just not my thing.

My thing is more about being heard and expressing myself. I write for blogs and co-author books with other writers. I write marketing copy for my website and have fun sending letters to people.

In another one of Tisha's group writing sessions, she gave us a "writing prompt" to help us move through some creativity in our writing. She guided us through a brief meditation and had us visualize being in a large house with many rooms and doors. Eventually, she led us into a room of our choosing. Basically, it was like, "Pick a room." A room in our life. A room in our past.

My mind went to this off campus college house bedroom. She then asked us this powerful question, "What in this room can you not see?" We opened our eyes and wrote for 10 minutes or so, and this is what poured out of me:

"I can't see my friend, Kent, who sometimes calls me on the line upstairs and my friends have to bang on the floor to prompt me to pick up the phone.

I can't see his beautiful face and his sweetest of smiles. I can't see how his back is hurting until he asks me to come over to give him a massage.

I can't see the night ahead when I come over to his apartment to find an empty chair in the middle of his living room. He asks me to sit in it in this dimly lit space and plays me a song that he thinks is our song.

I can't see the lyrics hitting me hard containing words like, 'Oh what a sweet surrender.'

I can't see that this night is one of the few vivid memories I now hold since his passing.

I can't see how he will swarm my thoughts for decades beyond his death. I can't see how this person has become all-consuming to me in the most precious of ways.

I can't see how much I'll miss him when he leaves too soon.

I can't see his son who he leaves behind who never got to meet him in person.

I can't see that 25 years later we will celebrate his son's engagement without him being present.

I can't see how much living in each and every moment is sacred until I realize that I want this moment back.

I can't see the power of my unfailing love for him. I can't see our future together as separate.

I can't see the truth within my grief.

I can't see myself fully.

There's such loneliness in grieving. I could sit here and tell you all about my friend, Kent. I could recount all these funny moments and describe all his best traits. But you could never know him the way I do."

This writing prompt sent me into another kind of writing, a more spiritual one. It made me realize that I have a completely different style of writing inside of me. I am grateful for this, and Tisha.

Coaching Tip:

Try giving yourself 15 minutes a week just to think and feel about your life.

Qualitarian Question:

When was the last time you allowed yourself to daydream?

PART NINE:
TYING IT ALL TOGETHER

32

Tying It All Together

Many of us are looking for a life that feels full of adventure and love. Some might be yearning for a life that feels like it's tied up in a big red bow. The truth is, neither of these scenarios is what life is really like.

A *Qualitarian* knows that life is messy. And it's the messiness that can make it magical. Our pain often leads to our healing. Our suffering may be a path to our joy.

I hear some people talk about how they choose their experiences. They choose everything. I believe this to a certain extent. But I think what we're choosing are the positive aspects of these experiences.

For example, maybe my soul wants to experience peace. How would I know what peace feels like unless I experience something uncomfortable like chaos? How would I know joy without first feeling sorrow?

We lean toward pleasure. We lean away from pain. *Qualitarians* understand that pain is the absence of pleasure just like hate is the absence of love. What if your spirit wanted to learn the lesson of forgiveness? Well, people would have to harm you in order for you to experience forgiving them.

Once you start honing this principle in your life, it's much easier to get un-stuck or to make a positive change for yourself. Maybe it's leaving a job you hate or ending a relationship that has become dysfunctional. Perhaps it's time to move out of your area or change the way you live.

We often think about making a change, don't we?

S-o-m-e-d-a-y:

I'll travel the world.

I'll write that book.

I'll spend more time doing what I love.

I'll break up with my partner who exhausts me.

I'll seek love by putting myself out there.

I'll rescue a pet.

I'll take more bubble baths.

I'll get a weekly massage.

I'll take daily walks.

I'll gain or lose that weight.

I'll start something or end something.

We live in someday-mode.

I had one of those standing-at-the-edge-of-a-cliff moments when I was 20. I was living with an abusive boyfriend in a very isolated area in the mountains of Southern California. We had dogs, so I had good company with them. But it became clear I was in a relationship that felt not only flat, but scary at times. I needed to leave. For the most part, I wanted to leave. Yet I didn't leave for a long time.

My family and friends told me to come back home. My best friend urged me to return to my former university to finish with him. I felt numb and paralyzed. I was very "in the moment" but the moments were boring and unsafe for me. I didn't yet understand the concept of qualitarianism.

Qualitarians look at moments and days and weeks and months and years, considering their quality. Instead, I was just surviving. I remember crocheting a lot of blankets in front of a lovely fire and chain smoking. The juxtaposition of me numbing myself with crocheting while watching beautiful flames in the fireplace was striking.

Getting unstuck was like ripping off a bandaid. One morning I recall feeling a strong sense of dread—like I needed to get out of there. It came on so suddenly that I simply left with two adult dogs and a litter of puppies. The thought in my head was, "If I don't leave right now, this could be a very bad day for me."

Whether we take the bandaid off slowly and quickly, what matters is that we're willing to look at the wound as it heals. We all have our own pace. Some of us like to take the elevator and others like to take the stairs. Some of us prefer a bath to a shower. Some of us like to slow wash the dishes by hand while others load the dishwasher for quick convenience.

The speed at which you make a change is totally up to you. No one is giving you a deadline. When it comes down to changes you're wanting to make, no one else cares the way you care. There's no referee and no magic wand.

Here's how *Qualitarians* make change in their lives. They seek and gain perspective about what life is like with or without the changes. They challenge themselves to ask and answer honestly where life is going and what kind of quality lies within it. Life is not worth living when it's full of mundane and uninspiring activity.

Making changes is about perception. Following through on changes is as simple as initiating actions. Self-awareness is not enough. Action is needed—sometimes with a flurry of activity, other times it may be more subtle. Action sometimes looks like an intention or a minimal movement. Noticing then acting. Observing then acting.

Maybe you notice that your body and mind can't stand to walk into work, especially on Monday mornings. What will you do with this "noticing?" What action will you take to better this situation? What single small step can you take? Trust me, small steps aren't so small when they lead you toward a better job. A better salary. Better health. Better workdays.

Feeling stuck is so uncomfortable. It's also debilitating. What I do when I'm feeling this way is to relax my thoughts. Relax my breath. Relax my emotions. Relax my body. I'm not a big meditator, so this may be one of the most meditative things I do.

One of my favorite writers, coaches and humans is Tama J. Kieves. She says, "Nothing needs to happen." This has become my favorite mantra. You see, it's not effort and exertion that gets us somewhere. It's surrendering. It's relaxing. It's being in a state of rest and realization.

Try this on the next time you feel stuck or need to make a life change. Try the way of the *Qualitarian*.

Coaching Tip:

Slow something down so slow that it forces you to be in the moment.

Qualitarian Question:

Instead of someday, when will you get to that important thing?

Conclusion

Living like a *Qualitarian* merely takes mindfulness and intention. It's the easiest thing you'll ever do—if you figure out what is most important to you. It's a matter of making decisions based on the quality of your life, moment to moment. It's about living life to its fullest without a lot of effort. It's simple to implement and gives immediate results.

Are you enjoying the quality of your experiences as they are happening? So often I see my coaching clients looking forward to something or recalling something but not actually "in it" when they're having the experience.

For example, my clients talk about going on vacation. "It's going to be so much fun!" is what they might say on the front end. "That was so fun!" is what they might say on the back end. But were they really truly having fun during the vacation? Sometimes not. Anticipating and reminiscing are the bookends of the experience, not the actual experience. You don't want to be a ghost in the experience.

Your outlook dictates your outcome. How are you perceiving your life?

You can change your circumstance or your perception. But the ultimate challenge is to change to a higher-quality circumstance or a higher-quality perception. What's the point of just changing to something different if it's of lesser or equal value?

A *Qualitarian* perceives life as a participant in it. What will you participate in next?

About the Author

Dez Stephens is the Founder and CEO of Radiant Coaches Academy (a division of Radiant Health Institute). Radiant Coaches Academy is a prominent international coach training school that certifies individuals to create vibrant, professional, private practices as holistic life coaches, wellness coaches and business coaches. She is a certified and credentialed coach, master trainer and marketing strategist. Dez is a humanitarian coach, a social entrepreneur, a people's advocate, and a planetary activist. She has coached professionally since 2005 and in 2012 she founded Radiant Coaches Academy, training and certifying over 600 students in 20 countries. In 2014, her training school earned the prestigious status of offering accredited hours through the International Coaching Federation (ICF). In 2017, ICF Tennessee honored her and her institute with the PRISM Award for the advancement of the coaching profession. Dez received her life coach certification from Guiding Mindful Change in 2005 and also holds a Professional Certified Coach (PCC) credential through ICF.